BREAK THE LANGUAGE BARRIER LEVEL 2
WWW.ELPRINCIPECENTRE.ORG
info@elprincipecentre.org

INTRODUCTION.

If you have chosen this book to help you learn Spanish you will have either already completed Level 1 or you will have felt that your level of Spanish was sufficient to start here at Level 2. Level 2 presumes knowledge and confidence with all aspects of the present tense, except for reflexive verbs which are dealt with here. Pronunciation tutorials are available on my YouTube channel https://youtu.be/fRH-q7OIGaU. Subscription is totally free.

If you find difficulty from the beginning, it would be a good idea to start with Level 1 for the good foundation it will give you. Here in Level 2 we will grapple with the most important past tenses, hopefully achieving a better understanding of the differences between them and when to use each one. My method of teaching Spanish is all about communication rather than grammatical perfection.

I have chosen the elements I believe are necessary to communicate effectively in Spanish. I do not delve into grammatical aspects that I feel will be too confusing and not necessary to get your point across. I concentrate on those components that will help successfully achieve whatever it is you are trying to do. However, I do like to refer to Break The Language Barrier Level 2 as the Pain Barrier, definitely the hardest Level in my series. ☺

However, I do not advocate "phrasebook" Spanish or "holiday" Spanish. With my method you will learn how to take the various components of the language in the simplest form possible and build your own phrases and questions to leave you confident in any situation. Spanish is a lovely, rich language spoken widely throughout the world. Most importantly, I hope you will enjoy working through this Level and feel sufficiently confident at the end to move on to Level 3. The past tenses can be notoriously difficult to get to grips with, and you will learn a lot about your own language as you work through them. It goes without saying that being able to use past tenses will expand your communication options immensely.

Accept with good grace that instant perfection is too much to expect, learn from your mistakes and be bold as you try to understand and make yourself understood, that is all part of the fun of learning a new language!!

Suerte!!

Vicki

Copyright© Vicki Marie Riley 1999-2023. All rights reserved.

BREAK THE LANGUAGE BARRIER LEVEL 2
WWW.ELPRINCIPECENTRE.ORG
info@elprincipecentre.org

INDEX

	Page Number
1. INTRODUCE YOURSELF.	3
2. REFLEXIVE VERBS.	4
3. REFLEXIVE VERBS IN CONTEXT.	10
4. REFLEXIVE VERBS- CONVERSATION PRACTICE.	12
5. THE PRESENT PERFECT.	13
6. THE PRESENT PERFECT IN CONTEXT.	16
7. DIRECT OBJECT PRONOUNS.	18
8. DIRECT OBJECT PRONOUNS IN CONTEXT.	21
9. THE BROKEN FLOWER VASE	24
10. CONVERSATION PRACTICE PRESENT PERFECT.	27
11. "SER" AND "ESTAR"- PRESENT TENSE AND PRESENT PERFECT	28
12. THE PRETERITE/ PAST SIMPLE TENSE- REGULAR VERBS.	31
13. PRETERITE TENSE - IRREGULAR VERBS.	34
14. "SER" AND "IR" - PRETERITE TENSE-THE "F" VERB.	36
15. CONVERSATION PRACTICE PRETERITE.	37
16. THE PRETERITE IN CONTEXT.	38
17. UNA TARDE INOLVIDABLE	40
18. COMPARISON OF "SER" AND "ESTAR" - PRETERITE.	42
19. "ALGO" / "NADA".	43
20. "ALGUIEN" / "NADIE".	46
21. THE IMPERFECT TENSE.	49
22. THE IMPERFECT TENSE IN CONTEXT.	51
23. IMPERFECT TENSE- CONVERSATION PRACTICE.	53
24. COMPARISON OF "SER" AND "ESTAR"-IMPERFECT TENSE.	54
25. VERB PRACTICE	56
26. COMPARISON OF TENSES	62
27. IDIOMATIC EXPRESSIONS.	65
28. LA ACTRÍZ ESTRELLA FUGAZ	66
29. THE PAST PERFECT/ PLUPERFECT	69
30. SUMMARY OF PAST TENSES	72
31. COMPARISON OF TENSES ENGLISH TO SPANISH 1	74
32. COMPARISON OF TENSES ENGLISH TO SPANISH 2	76
33. PRACTICE OF PAST TENSES "ADIÓS MARÍA"	78
34. TRANSLATION FROM ENGLISH TO SPANISH-MIXED TENSES.	80
27. POSTSCRIPT.	84
28. KEY TO "TOP TIPS".	85
29. ANSWERS.	86

Copyright© Vicki Marie Riley 1999-2023. All rights reserved.

BREAK THE LANGUAGE BARRIER LEVEL 2
WWW.ELPRINCIPECENTRE.ORG
info@elprincipecentre.org

1. INTRODUCE YOURSELF.

If you are ready for Level 2, you should be able to ask and answer the following questions in Spanish. If you have problems with these, please go back through Level 1 to refresh before starting this course.

PRACTICE A: Translate these questions into Spanish and answer them

1. What´s your name?
2. Where do you live?
3. Do you live in a house or an apartment?
4. What is your house like?
5. Are you married?
6. Do you have any children?
7. How old are they?
8. Where do they live?
9. What do you do in your spare time?
10. How many languages do you speak?
11. Why is Spanish important for you?
12. When is your birthday?
13. Why do you want to learn Spanish?
14. Where do you work?
15. What do you like most about Spain?
16. What do you like least?
17. Do you like Spanish food?
18. Do you understand Spanish verbs?
19. Why must you eat vegetables?
20. Who do you remember most from school?
21. Where do you want to go on holiday?
22. Where is your car?
23. Who is your best friend?
24. Where do you normally go on Sundays?
25. Where are you from?
26. Are you happy?
27. What are you like?
28. What do you do in the evening?
29. What do you drink in a restaurant?
30. Do you drink a lot of coffee?

2. REFLEXIVE VERBS.

A reflexive verb is something one does to one self such as – to wash oneself or to dress oneself etc. These verbs are used with reflexive pronouns that denote which person is carrying out the action.

E.g.   I wash **myself.**
       You dress **yourself.**

Most verbs can be used in a reflexive way, **"to wash"** and **"to wash oneself"** are both valid verb forms, and this is true in Spanish also. To make a verb reflexive in Spanish we add **"se"** to the end of the infinitive. When we conjugate the verb, this converts into different pronouns representing the different persons and changes its position to immediately in front of the main verb. Let´s look at how this works using the verb **"llamar"**- to call, which in it´s reflexive form becomes **"to call oneself"** and therefore is how we speak about names in Spanish.

Llamar	To call	Llamarse	To call oneself, to be called
Llamo	I call	Me llamo	I call myself
Llamas	you call	Te llamas	You call yourself
Llama	he/she/it calls	Se llama	He/she/it calls him/her/itself,
Llamamos	we call	Nos llamamos	We call ourselves
Llamáis	you(s) call	Os llamáis	You(s) call yourselves
Llaman	they call	Se llaman	They call themselves

Os llamáis-You(s) call yourselves, you(s) are called.
Se llaman-They call themselves, they are called.

E.g- Llamo a Juan cada noche- I call Juan every night.
     Me llamo Vicki- I am called Vicki (literally I call myself Vicki).

See how the reflexive pronoun changes the meaning of the verb.

PRACTICE A: Find the English meaning to the following reflexive verbs and conjugate them as above.

1. Levantarse -

2. Despertarse -
(dipthong "e" to "ie")

3. Pintarse -

4. Lavarse -

5. Ducharse-

6. Acostarse-
(dipthong "o"
to "ue")

7. Afeitarse

8. Vestirse
(dipthong "e" to "i")

9. Ponerse

10. Peinarse

PRACTICE B: Practice reading the text below out loud. Then pick out all the <u>reflexive verbs</u> (12) and give the English meaning in the box below.

Me llamo Pedro Martínez y soy mecánico. Todos los días me levanto a las siete. Voy al cuarto de baño, me ducho, me afeito, y me peino. Después, vuelvo a mi habitación y me visto.

Mi hermano duerme en la misma habitación. Casi siempre se despierta más tarde. Es muy vago. A veces está en la cama hasta las diez. No trabaja. Va al Instituto donde estudia pero a veces se queda en cama porque las clases son aburridas.

Mis padres también se levantan a las siete. Mi madre prepara el desayuno y mi padre lee el periódico. A las siete y media desayunamos y después salimos de la casa. Mi padre va a la oficina, yo al taller, mi hermano al Instituto y mi madre se va de compras.

Por la noche nos reunimos todos de nuevo. Cenamos, vemos la televisión y luego nos acostamos.

BREAK THE LANGUAGE BARRIER LEVEL 2
WWW.ELPRINCIPECENTRE.ORG
info@elprincipecentre.org

Verb	Infinitive	English Meaning	Meaning in context
1. me llamo	llamarse	To call oneself	I call myself
2.			
3.			
4.			
5.			
6.			
7.			
8.			
9.			
10.			
11.			
12.			

PRACTICE C: Translate the text into English.

PRACTICE D: Translate these questions into Spanish then answer them in Spanish. The answers are all in the text.

1. What time does Pedro get up?
2. What does he do in the bathroom?
3. What does he do when he returns to his bedroom?
4. Who sleeps in the same room?
5. Does his brother work?
6. Why does he sometimes stay in bed?
7. Who also gets up at seven?
8. What does his mother do while his father reads the paper?
9. What do they do after breakfast?
10. Where does his mother go?
11. What do they do in the evening?
12. What do they do after having dinner and watching the television?

PRACTICE E: What is your daily routine? Write about it using as many reflexive verbs as possible.

Top Tips!!

---

1. Placement of reflexive pronouns:

Reflexive pronouns need to be placed in front of a conjugated verb but if there is an infinitive or gerund ("ing" word) in the sentence it can be tagged on the end. If there are both a conjugated verb and either of the above in a sentence you can place it where feels more comfortable for you.

E.g. Me ducho todos los días- I shower every day.
   Cada día (me) tengo que duchar(me) - Every day I have to shower.
   (Me) Estoy duchando(me) - I am having a shower.

---

2. Quedar/se:

"Quedar/se" is an interesting verb with varied meanings depending on context. Here are some examples but be aware it is not an exhaustive list!!

1. Quiero quedar con él mañana- I want to meet him tomorrow.
2. Los zapatos te quedan muy bien- The shoes really suit you.
3. Se quedan en casa cada sábado noche- They stay at home every Saturday night.
4. No me queda azúcar- I have no sugar left.
5. Quedamos contentos con las reformas- We are happy with the building work.

3. REFLEXIVE VERBS IN CONTEXT.

Every night María **goes to bed** at 11.30. She falls asleep quickly and she never has nightmares. She wakes up at 7.00 a.m but never gets up until 7.15. She goes off to the bathroom where she brushes her teeth and looks at herself in the mirror. Sometimes she bathes, but usually she showers because it is faster and she feels cleaner.

Afterwards, she brushes her hair and dries her hair. María gets dressed and puts on her make-up, then she goes off to the kitchen where she makes herself a coffee, sits down and reads the paper for 10 minutes. Then she goes off to work.

PRACTICE A: There are 21 verbs in total in this text, reflexive and non-reflexive. Pick them out and put them in the box below following the example that has been done for you.

VERB IN CONTEXT	INFINITIVE	SPANISH
1. Goes to bed	To go to bed	Acostarse (dipthong-"o" to "ue")
2.		
3.		
4.		
5.		
6.		
7.		
8.		
9.		
10.		
11.		
12.		
13.		
14.		
15.		

16.		
17.		
18.		
19.		
20.		
21.		

PRACTICE B: Translate the whole text into Spanish.

PRACTICE C: Translate these questions into Spanish and answer in Spanish. The answers are all in the text.

1. What time does María go to bed every night?
2. Does she have nightmares?
3. What time does she wake up every morning?
4. Does she get up at that time?
5. What does she do in the bathroom?
6. Why does she usually shower?
7. What does she do afterwards?
8. What does she do in the kitchen?
9. What does she do then?
10. What time do you normally get up?

NB-Placement of reflexive pronouns: The reflexive pronouns "**me**", "**te**", "**se**", "**nos**", "**os**" and "**se**" are normally placed in front of a conjugated verb
E.g. **Me** levanto a las siete- *I get up at seven.*
They can only go after an infinitive, where they are tagged on as part of the word.
If the sentence contains both a conjugated verb and an infinitive you can chose where to place it:
E.g. **(Nos)** queremos levantar**(nos)** a las siete- *We want to get up at seven.*

4. REFLEXIVE VERBS- CONVERSATION PRACTICE.

PRACTICE A: Find the English meaning of these reflexive verbs.

1. lavarse.
2. sentirse.
3. ponerse nervioso.
4. acostarse.
5. quitarse.
6. enfermarse.
7. ponerse.
8. preocuparse.
9. casarse.
10. enfadarse.
11. ducharse.
12. bañarse.
13. cepillarse.
14. llamarse.
15. levantarse.

PRACTICE B: Use them to translate the questions below. Practice asking and answering them with a friend.

1. What do you call yourself?
2. What time do you normally get up?
3. What time do you normally go to bed?
4. Do you prefer to shower or to bathe?
5. When do you get angry?
6. Why do you worry?
7. How do you feel today?
8. When do you become nervous?
9. Do you take off your shoes in the house?
10. Do you get ill often?
11. How many times a day do you brush your teeth?
12. Where do people get married in Spain?
13. Do you wash your hair every day?
14. What clothes do you put on in the winter?

5. THE PRESENT PERFECT.

The "present perfect" is what is known as a compound tense. In other words it is formed by 2 separate verbs rather than one. It translates to the English to "have done something".

It straddles two time zones as we use it to talk about actions that started in the past but continue into the present.
E.g. I have lived in Spain for 5 years- *He vivido en España durante 5 años.*

Therefore, we know that this person started living in Spain in the past but is still living there.

We also use it to talk about recent actions, things we have only just done.
E.g. Have you eaten your lunch yet?- *¿Has comido ya?*

How do we construct it in English?

In English we first use the verb "to have" in the present tense:

INFINITIVE	TO HAVE
1st person singular	I have
2nd person singular	You have
3rd person singular	He/she/it has
1st person plural	We have
2nd person plural	You (s) have
3rd person plural	They have

We then add what is called the "past participle" to describe what we "have done". Regular past participles in English are formed by ending the verb with "ed", such as **"wanted"**, **"dreamed"**, **"studied"**, **"kissed"**, **"loved"**, **"listened"**, etc. However, there are plenty of irregular past participles such as **"eaten"**, **"drunk"**, **"written"**, **"been"**, **"had"**, **"taken"**, **"broken"**, etc.

How do we construct it in Spanish?

We do not use the verb **"tener"** that normally means **"to have"** to construct the first part. We use a special verb **"haber"** that is used to specifically to construct tenses. It is conjugated as follows:

BREAK THE LANGUAGE BARRIER LEVEL 2

WWW.ELPRINCIPECENTRE.ORG

info@elprincipecentre.org

INFINITIVE	TO HAVE	HABER
1st person singular	I have	he
2nd person singular	You have	has
3rd person singular	He/she/it has	ha
1st person plural	We have	hemos
2nd person plural	You (s) have	habéis
3rd person plural	They have	han

Regular Spanish **past participles** are formed as follows:

"**Ar**" verbs- remove the "ar" and add "ado". E.g. **hablado**- spoken
"**Er**" verbs- remove the "er" **and add** "ido", E.g. **aprendido**- learnt
"**Ir**" verbs- same as "**er**" verbs. E.g. **vivido**-lived

PRACTICE A: Translate the following into Spanish. All the verbs used have <u>REGULAR</u> past participles formed as described above.

1. How long have you worked here?
2. Today I have washed the car and cleaned the house, and my husband has watched the television.
3. This year we have read lots of different books.
4. This week she has paid 200 euros for books for school.
5. Have you (s) eaten yet?
6. Where are they? They have gone to the shops.
7. He has drunk too much beer and eaten too much chocolate.
8. I have bought my clothes here for 13 years.
9. Have you washed the dishes yet?
10. We have studied a lot of Spanish this month.

Just like in English, **IRREGULAR** past participles have no pattern and simply have to be learnt.

PRACTICE B: Here are a group of verbs that have irregular participles. What is the English participle for each verb? The first one has been done for you.

1. Escribir - to write - escrito - written.
2. Hacer -   - hecho -
3. Romper -   - roto -
4. Ver -   - visto -

Copyright© Vicki Marie Riley 1999-2023. All rights reserved.

5. Volver -   - vuelto -
6. Decir -   - dicho -
7. Abrir -   - abierto -
8. Morir -   - muerto -
9. Poner -   - puesto -
10. Cubrir -   - cubierto -
11. Freir -   - frito -

PRACTICE C: Use the verbs to translate these sentences.

1. How many letters have you written?
2. Have you seen Juan?
3. Who has broken the window?
4. What have you done?
5. What has Pedro said to you?
6. I have fried two eggs this morning.
7. The king has died.
8. Someone has opened the windows.
9. They haven't returned yet.
10. Where have you(s) put the keys?
11. The snow has covered the mountains.

PRACTICE D: ¿Qué has hecho esta semana? What have you done this week? Translate the questions below into Spanish and then answer with a full answer in both positive and negative.

E.g. Have you cleaned the car this week? ¿Has lavado el coche esta semana?
Si, he lavado el coche esta semana. / No, no he lavado el coche esta semana.

1. Have you seen a film ?
2. Have you written a letter?
3. Have you read a book?
4. Have you told a lie?
5. Have you fried a hamburger?
6. Have you eaten pasta?
7. Have you drunk wine?
8. Have you broken anything?
9. Have you spoken Spanish with anyone?
10. Have you done your homework?

6. THE PRESENT PERFECT IN CONTEXT.

PRACTICE A: Practice reading this text out loud.

Hola Ana

He llegado en Manchester hace solo dos días y ya tengo mil cosas para contarte. Cómo sabes, vivo con una familia inglesa muy simpática, especialmente el hijo David que además es muy guapo.
Esta mañana he tenido mi primera clase de inglés. Mi profesora se llama Carol y es rubia, alta y muy maja. Por la tarde hemos ido al Museo de Manchester con el profesor de historia Alan, que es bajo, calvo y un poco serio y hemos visitado todas las salas de Egipto.
Después, hemos estado en el Centro tomando algunas tapas en un restaurante español. He pasado todo el día hablando en inglés, ha sido estupendo, aunque todavía tengo algunos problemas en escuchar a la gente. Ahora me acuesto porque estoy muy cansada.

Un abrazo, cuídate

Maite

PRACTICE B: Pick out the 22 verbs in this text. Use them to complete the verb identification table below as per the example.

VERB	INFINITIVE	ENGLISH	TENSE	PERSON
1. He llegado	llegar	To arrive	Present perfect	1st person singular
2.				
3.				
4.				
5.				
6.				
7.				
8.				
9.				
10.				
11.				
12.				
13.				
14.				

15.				
16.				
17.				
18.				
19.				
20.				
21.				
22.				

PRACTICE C: *Translate the text into English.*

PRACTICE D: *Translate these questions into Spanish and answer in Spanish.*

1. When has Maite arrived in Manchester?
2. Who does she live with?
3. What has she had this morning?
4. What is her teacher called?
5. What is she like?
6. Where have they been in the afternoon?
7. What is the history teacher like?
8. What have they visited?
9. Where have they been then?
10. How has she spent all day?
11. What problems does she still have?
12. Why is she going to bed now?

Top Tips!!

---

3. Ending a letter or email in Spanish.

Here are some informal endings that can be used on emails or letters:
1. Un beso/besos- a kiss/ kisses.
2. Un abrazo/ abrazos- a hug/ hugs.
3. Cuídate- look after yourself.
4. Saludos- best wishes.
5. Tengo ganas de verte- I look forward to seeing you.

7. DIRECT OBJECT PRONOUNS.

What is a Direct Object Pronoun? (DOP)
We use DOP s rather than repeating the full names of people or things. Lets take this simple sentence- **"I have seen John."**
If we grammatically dissect this sentence, the subject is "I" (person or thing performing the action), the verb is "have seen" (the action), and the direct object is "John", i.e. who or what the action is done to. We would use a direct object pronoun if we wished to continue to talk about John without constantly repeating his name.

E.g "I have seen John. I have seen **him** today .
"Him" is the DOP used to avoid saying- "I have seen **John**. I have seen **John** today."
He visto a Juan. **Lo** he visto hoy.
Here are the DOPs in Spanish alongside their English equivalent.

English	Spanish
me	me
you	te
him/her/it	lo(m)/la(f)
us	nos
you(s)	os
them	los(m)/las(f)

(In Spanish, DOP´s are placed either directly before a conjugated verb or tagged on the end of an infinitive.)

PRACTICE A: TRANSLATE INTO SPANISH. SOME ARE PRESENT TENSE, SOME ARE PRESENT PERFECT.

1. He has given it to María.
2. He hasn't given it to María.
3. They want to see you(s).
4. They haven't seen them (f) this week.
5. She has looked for him all day.
6. I clean it every week (f).
7. Have you understood it?
8. He has seen us.
9. John calls him.
10. They say it all the time.
11. He has taken her to the airport.
12. I have taken it home.

13. He can´t sell it (f)
14. Have you seen it (f)?
15. We have forgotten them.
16. They have forgotten us.
17. She has bought it this week.
18. They have painted it. (f)
19. He hasn't done it.
20. Have you done it?
21. They haven't written them (f).
22. I understand him
23. He kisses her
24. They invite us.
25. I see them.

PRACTICE B: TRANSLATE INTO SPANISH.

1. Paco loves her.
2. I need you.
3. He looks for them (f).
4. They visit us.
5. Who knows her?
6. They have waited for us a long time.
7. You believe me.
8. I wait for you(s).
9. She tells us.
10. The boys have seen me.
11. I look at him.
12. They choose you.
13. I don't hear him.
14. They don´t want it. (f)
15. We can´t see her.
16. I don´t visit them often.
17. She doesn´t want to do it.
18. I have put it (f) on the table.
19. I don´t want them here.
20. You(s) do it every day.
21. You know it.
22. He finds it difficult.
23. We hate them.
24. I have seen them (f) today.
25. You take them to the airport every time.

Top Tips!!

4. "Saber" y "Conocer":

There are 2 verbs "to know" in Spanish, "saber" and "conocer". "Saber" is used for knowing information, facts or how to do something.

E.g. 1. Sé que mañana es su cumpleaños- I know that tomorrow is his/her birthday.
    2. ¿Cuánto tiempo has sabido nadar? How long have you known how to swim?
    3. ¿Sabes dónde está la farmacia?-Do you know where the Chemist is?

"Conocer" is used to talk about being acquainted with people or places. It can also mean "meet".

E.g. 1. He conocido a Juan durante muchos años- I have known Juan for many years.
    2. ¿Conoces España muy bien?- Are you very familiar with Spain?
    3. ¿Has conocido a muchos españoles?- Have you met many Spanish people?

8. DIRECT OBJECT PRONOUNS IN CONTEXT.

<u>I want</u> to visit my sister because I haven´t seen her for more than two weeks. I need to call her because I think my boyfriend has left me. I have called him on the telephone, I have been to his house, but I don´t know where he is. I have looked for him in his local bar, in his office and at his parent´s house but I haven´t been able to find him.

His brother says he has gone on holiday, but he hasn´t said anything to me. He says he has wanted to go to Spain for a long time and he thinks that he is there now. I want to talk to my sister as she has always given me good advice and I need it now. I have to see her and take her to lunch in order to chat.

I haven´t argued with him so I don´t understand why he has left me without saying anything. I have left my sunglasses at his house and I need them for my holidays next week. I have also left my black handbag there and I need it for a party on Saturday night. If I can´t get it my boyfriend´s brother can get it for me. Also my sunglasses, he can get them for me also.

PRACTICE A: Pick out the verbs in this text (45) and complete the verb identification table below as per the example.

VERB	INFINITIVE	SPANISH	TENSE	PERSON
1. I want	To want	querer	present	1st p. sing.
2.				
3.				
4.				
5.				
6.				
7.				
8.				
9.				
10.				
11.				
12.				
13.				
14.				
15.				
16.				

17.					
18.					
19.					
20.					
21.					
22.					
23.					
24.					
25.					
26.					
27.					
28.					
29.					
30.					
31.					
32.					
33.					
34.					
35.					
36.					
37.					
38.					
39.					
40.					
41.					
42.					
43.					
44.					
45.					

PRACTICE B: Translate into Spanish.

PRACTICE C: Translate these questions into Spanish and answer in Spanish.

1. Why does she want to visit her sister?
2. Why does she need to call her?
3. Where has she looked for her boyfriend?
4. What does her boyfriend´s brother say?
5. Why does she want to talk to her sister?

6. Where does she need to take her and why?
7. Has she argued with him?
8. What has she left at his house?
9. Why does she need them?
10. What has she also left there?
11. Why does she need it?
12. Who can get them for her?

Top Tips!!

5. "Salir" and "dejar":

1. "Salir"-To leave (exit) from a place:
E.g. Hemos salido ya de la fiesta-We have already left the party.
    El tren sale a las 12 para Alicante- The train leaves at 12 for Alicante.

Also means "to go out":
E.g. Salimos todas las noches- We go out every night.
    Han salido a trabajar- They have left for work.

2. "Dejar". To leave something/one behind:
E.g. Han dejado su coche en el playa- They have left their car on the beach.
    Lo ha dejado- She has left him.

Also means to leave someone/thing alone:
E.g. Nunca me dejas en paz - You never leave me in peace.

Also means to stop doing something, give something up:
E.g. He decidido dejar de fumar- I have decided to give up smoking.

And also to leave/let someone to do something:
E.g. Os dejo decidir- I´ll let you(s) decide.
    Mi madre no me deja ir solo- My mother won´t let me go alone.

9. THE BROKEN FLOWER VASE

PRACTICE A: Find the verbs and translate this text into Spanish

It is a nice spring afternoon and Mr. Martinez has returned from the office. This afternoon he has to prepare dinner because his wife has gone to Barcelona to spend a few days with her parents. Pedro and Maria have returned before their father. Maria has already started to prepare dinner and Pedro has laid the table. Mr. Martinez has opened the door of the living room and has gone in, but he hasn't sat down because he can't find his newspaper. **(15)**

Mr. Martinez - "Pedro, have you seen my newspaper? I have forgotten where I have put it".
Pedro - "I haven't seen it Dad. Perhaps you have left it in the kitchen."
Maria - "What are you looking for?"
Mr. Martinez - "My newspaper. I want to read a little before dinner."
Maria - "You have left it on the small table. Do you see it? On the left of that blue vase over there."
Mr. Martinez - "Ah, yes, I see it. Thank you Maria." **(11)**

He goes to get it, but he slips and bangs against the table, the vase falls to the floor.
Maria - "Dad what have you done, is the vase broken?"
Mr. Martinez - "Yes, I have broken it."
Maria - "Oh Dad, mum has always said that it is her favourite vase. It is a present from her aunt Lourdes"
Mr. Martinez - "Let's see. Your mother returns on Friday. We have four days to find another one" **(15)**

The next day Mr. Martinez explains to his friend Jordi what he has done. He wants to help him and says that there is a shop in the City Centre where they sell this type of ceramics.
"I haven't had any luck" he says to Jordi the next day when he returns from the office. "They have sold all of them".
His children haven't had any luck either. They have visited many shops without finding anything.
"Juan has helped us", says Pedro, "but we haven't found anything." **(16)**

Mrs. Martinez returns from Barcelona on Friday and the others go to the station to greet her. With her she has her suitcase and a large parcel. She doesn't want to open it before arriving home. On the way to the house her husband explains how he has broken the vase. She says nothing. In the house she puts the parcel on the table, she takes out the scissors and cuts the cord around the parcel. She opens it and takes out another vase.

"I have bought it in Barcelona" she says, "so I forgive you". **(18)**

PRACTICE B: Translate these questions into Spanish and answer in Spanish

1. What is the afternoon like?
2. From where has Mr Martinez returned?
3. Why does he have to prepare dinner this evening?
4. Who has returned before him?
5. Who has already started to prepare dinner?
6. What has Pedro done?
7. Why hasn't Mr Martinez sat down?
8. Has Pedro seen it?
9. Where has he left it?
10. What happens when he goes to get it?
11. Is the vase broken?
12. When does Mrs Martinez return?
13. To who does Mr Martinez explain what he has done?

14. Where is there a shop that sells this kind of ceramics?

15. Has he had any luck?

16. Have the children had any luck?

17. Who has helped them?

18. Who do they greet at the station?

19. What does she have with her?

20. What does her husband explain on the way to the house?

21. What does she say?

22. What does she do in the house?

23. What does she take out?

24. Where has she bought it?

10. CONVERSATION PRACTICE PRESENT PERFECT- "EVER"/"ALGUNA VEZ".

In Spanish we use "alguna vez" for "ever" as in when in English we ask if someone has "ever" done something.
E.g. Have you **ever** written a book?- ¿Has escrito un libro **alguna** vez?
Notice the word order is different.
The two possible replies are:
Si, he escrito un libro alguna vez. (affirmative)
No, no he escrito un libro **ninguna vez** or No, **nunca** he escrito un libro. (negative)

PRACTICE A: Translate these questions into Spanish and answer in Spanish, practice with a friend if possible.

1. Have you ever been in Mexico?
2. Have you ever seen a UFO?
3. Have you ever seen a ghost?
4. Have you ever lived in another country?
5. Have you ever seen a robbery?
6. Have you ever won a prize?
7. Have you ever missed a flight or a train?
8. Have you ever lost all your money?
9. Have you ever had an accident?
10. Have you ever studied German?
11. Have you ever had a dog?
12. Have you ever met anyone famous?
13. Have you ever been to the United States?
14. Have you ever done anything silly?
15. Have you ever written a poem?
16. Have you ever cooked for more than 20 people?
17. Have you ever bought anything really expensive?
18. Have you ever bought a red car?
19. Have you ever spoken to a stranger on a train?
20. Have you ever told a lie?

11. "SER" AND "ESTAR"- THE 2 VERBS "TO BE"- PRESENT TENSE AND PRESENT PERFECT.

As we saw in Level 1, in English, we are lucky enough to only have to deal with one verb "to be". However, in Spanish, we have to think a little about what we "are" before deciding whether "ser" or "estar" are appropriate. Now we have also moved into the a different tense so there is even more to consider.

PRESENT TENSE

TO BE	SER	ESTAR
I am	(yo) soy	(yo) estoy
You are	(tú) eres	(tú) estás
He, she, it is	(él, ella) es	(él, ella) está
We are	(nosotros, as) somos	(nosotros, as) estamos
You(s) are	(vosotros, as) sois	(vosotros, as) estáis
They are	(Ellos, ellas) son	(Ellos, ellas) están

PRESENT PERFECT

TO HAVE BEEN	SER	ESTAR
I have been	(yo) he sido	(yo) he estado
You have been	(tú) has sido	(tú) has estado
He, she, it has been	(él, ella) ha sido	(él, ella) ha estado
We have been	(nosotros, as) hemos sido	(nosotros, as) hemos estado
You(s) have been	(vosotros, as) habéis sido	(vosotros, as) habéis estado
They have been	(Ellos, ellas) han sido	(Ellos, ellas) han estado

USES OF "SER"

"Ser" is commonly known as the "permanent" verb to be, in that we use it to describe what we always are, things that do not change. Therefore "ser" is used to describe our identity, our nationality and origin, intrinsic physical appearance or personality traits. However, our profession or what we do is an exception as ser is used for this although it quite clearly can change. "Ser" is also used for time and possession.

USES OF "ESTAR"

"Estar", in turn, is commonly known as the "temporary" verb to be, describing what we are at this moment in time but not neccesarily something that is an intrinsic part of our make-up. Therefore we use estar to describe our mood, emotions, temporary states and conditions of things or people. Also our marital status and even if something is alive or dead.

The difference between **"el cielo _es_ azul"** (el thee-el-oh es ah-thul) -the sky is blue, and **"el cielo _está_ azul"**, also the sky is blue, is that when we use **"ser"** we are describing a universal truth, whereas **"estar"** speaks of the current state of something or someone. As always, there is an exception... Whenever we are talking about the situation or where someone or something is, we **ALWAYS ALWAYS** use "estar", whether it is there at the moment or always there. Just remember **LOCATION, LOCATION, LOCATION** always means "estar"!

Here we can see how important the distinction is between the two, as it can change the meaning of your sentence.

If I say, **"Juan es simpático"**- Juan is nice- I am using the verb **"ser"** so I am saying he is an intrinsically nice person
If I say **"Juan está simpático hoy"**- I am saying he is nice today, the use of the verb **"estar"** suggests he is not normally so.

"El plátano es amarillo"- the banana is yellow- yellow is the accepted "normal" colour of a banana.
"El plátano está negro"- this particular banana is black- **"estar"** is used because it is not the universally accepted colour.

"Carmen es triste"- Carmen is sad- the use of **"ser"** tells us she is a "sad" person generally
"Carmen está triste"- the use of **"estar"** tells us this is just her current feeling or emotion rather than a trait of her personality.

PRACTICE A: Translate the following (using verb "ser" only).

1. We are English.
2. The table is square.
3. They have been teachers for 20 years.
4. She has always been tall.
5. They are from Spain.

6. Who is Juan?
7. I have never been his friend.
8. Are they Spanish?
9. Have you(s) ever been a student?
10. When is the class?

PRACTICE B: Translate the following (using verb "estar" only).

1. We have been in England.
2. The table is dirty.
3. Are you tired?
4. Are you(s) happy?
5. She is in the garden.
6. They have been ill.
7. I have been very sad.
8. Paris is in France.
9. The children are ill.
10. This apple is black.

PRACTICE C: Translate the following (choose whether to use "ser" or "estar").

1. Where are you from?
2. Where have they been?
3. Where is my car?
4. The ball is red.
5. Jordi and Maria have been very tired today.
6. How are you?
7. What´s Pedro like?
8. Who are we with?
9. The cats have been on the terrace all morning.
10. The house is dirty.
11. José has always been a very good-looking man.
12. Maria and Belén are blonde.
13. Manuel and Begoña have been lawyers in the city since 2005.
14. He has been my best friend for 10 years.
15. When is the Spanish class?

12. THE PRETERITE/ SIMPLE PAST TENSE-REGULAR VERBS.

The Preterite, or Simple Past Tense is used for singular, completed actions in the past, at a specific point in time. In English, anything we 'did'.

E.g. I ate in a restaurant last night- **Comí en un restaurante anoche.**

In English, we conjugate regular verbs by adding "ed", such as "to walk" below.

PRESENT TENSE	PRETERITE/ SIMPLE PAST
I walk	I walked
You walk	You walked
He/she/it walks	He/she/it walked
We walk	We walked
You (s) walk	You (s) walked
They walk	They walked

Note that the conjugation is the same for all persons.

In Spanish we first do the same as we do for the present tense in that we remove the "ar", "er" and "ir" to give us the root or stem of the verb, then add on a different ending that represents each of the different grammatical persons.

The conjugation of regular verbs is as follows: -

"AR"-pasar-
to pass/happen
(passed/happened)

"ER"-aprender-
to learn
(learnt)

"IR"- escribir-
to write
(wrote)

pas / **é**
pas / **aste**
pas / **ó**
pas / **amos**
pas / **asteis**
pas / **aron**

aprend / **í**
aprend / **iste**
aprend / **ió**
aprend / **imos**
aprend / **isteis**
aprend / **ieron**

escrib / **í**
escrib / **iste**
escrib / **ió**
escrib / **imos**
escrib / **isteis**
escrib / **ieron**

Note that "ER" and "IR" verbs share the same endings.

It is always used with the following expressions:

yesterday : ayer.
last night : anoche.
the day before yesterday : anteayer.
last week : la semana pasada.
last month : el mes pasado.
last year: el año pasado.

PRACTICE A: Here are 10 other verbs that are regular in this tense. Find out their meaning and conjugate them in the boxes provided.

1. MIRAR 2. HABLAR. 3. VER. 4. ENVIAR. 5. VIVIR. 6. COMER.
7. BEBER. 8. LIMPIAR. 9. RECIBIR. 10. ESCUCHAR.

(no accents for "ver")

1. mirar	To watch, look at	2. hablar	to	3. ver	to
mir	é				
mir					
mir					
mir					
mir					
mir					

4. enviar		5. vivir		6. comer	

7. beber		8. limpiar		9. recibir	

10. escuchar	

PRACTICE B: Use the verbs to translate these sentences into Spanish.

1. Last night I spoke to Juan.
2. I saw the doctor yesterday.
3. We listened to a lot of Spanish last month.
4. The day before yesterday I received a letter.
5. We looked at a lot of houses in France in the summer.
6. You had lunch in a restaurant.
7. I cleaned the house yesterday.
8. I lived in England in 1988.
9. You(s) drank beer at the party last night.
10. We sent lots of emails yesterday.
11. Did you(s) see the storm the day before yesterday?
12. They cleaned the car last week.
13. He danced at the disco on Friday night.
14. She drank too much wine at the weekend.
15. Did you buy anything on Saturday?
16. Who did you speak to at the party?

13. PRETERITE TENSE - IRREGULAR VERBS.

Here are a group of common verbs that have irregular stems, and share a set of endings between them. However there are some anomalies, which are highlighted.

1. hacer- hic (3rd person singular stem is "hiz").
2. poner-pus
3. poder-pud
4. saber-sup
5. estar- estuv
6. dar -d (takes the endings for regular "er" verbs without accents).
7. tener – tuv
8. *decir – dij (3rd person plural "eron" not "ieron").
9. *conducir-conduj (3rd person plural "eron" not "ieron").
10. *traer- traj (3rd person plural "eron" not "ieron").
11. querer -quis
12. venir- vin

Endings – e, iste, o, imos, isteis, ieron .

PRACTICE A: Conjugate the verbs in the preterite/simple past tense and find what they mean in English.

1. hacer -
2. poner -
3. poder -
4. saber -
5. estar -
6. dar -

7. tener-	8. decir-	9. conducir-

10. traer-	11. querer -	12. venir-

PRACTICE B: Use The verbs to translate the following sentences.

1. What did you do last night?
2. Where did you put the newspaper?
3. He gave Carmen a present.
4. We drove here yesterday.
5. They came to Spain in August.
6. She wanted to buy the house last year.
7. In 1999, I had my first child.
8. The waiter brought the menu to the table.
9. We couldn´t sleep last night.
10. What did you(s) say to Pablo?
11. Did you know how to open the door?
12. Where were you on Friday at 4 o´clock?
13. Why did you give Juan the key?
14. I drove to the market.
15. They brought us a bottle of wine.
16. You(s) couldn´t do it.
17. She put the paper in the rubbish bin.
18. I admit it. I did it.
19. She made herself (reflexive) a cup of coffee yesterday afternoon.
20. They put on (reflexive) their hats and gloves (in order) to go to the park.

14. SER AND IR - PRETERITE/ PAST SIMPLE TENSE-THE "F" VERB.

The two most irregular verbs in the past simple are SER and IR – which in this tense are the same in Spanish:

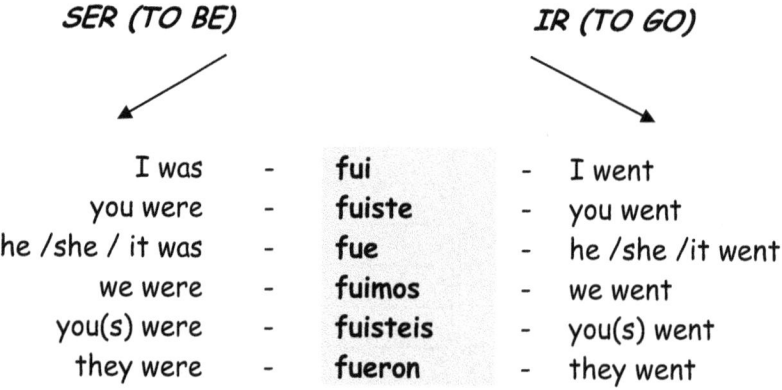

SER (TO BE)		IR (TO GO)
I was - **fui** -		I went
you were - **fuiste** -		you went
he /she / it was - **fue** -		he /she /it went
we were - **fuimos** -		we went
you(s) were - **fuisteis** -		you(s) went
they were - **fueron** -		they went

E.g. **Fue** buen día ayer- It was a good day yesterday.
   Fue al cine ayer - He went to the cinema yesterday.

The context will tell us which verb it is, also remember that "ir" is normally accompanied by "a" as we are normally going "to" somewhere.

PRACTICE A: Translate these sentences into Spanish.

1. I was a student in 1979.
2. I went off to the shops yesterday. (reflexive)
3. Did you go to the party last night?
4. The house was cheap 5 years ago.
5. Last Saturday they went to Juan's house.
6. The class was very interesting.
7. Did you(s) go to the market on Saturday?
8. We went home at 8 o' clock.
9. Who was the best student yesterday?
10. Pedro and Maria were husband and wife for 5 years, but they never went to England.

15. CONVERSATION PRACTICE PRETERITE/ SIMPLE PAST.

PRACTICE A: Translate these questions into Spanish and answer in Spanish. Practice them with a friend if possible.

1. What did you do last night?
2. What time did you get up last Sunday?
3. Where did you go the day before yesterday?
4. Who did you speak to on Saturday?
5. What did your family give you for your last birthday?
6. What film did you see last month?
7. What did you put on yesterday?
8. When did you have your first Spanish class?
9. What time did you have dinner last night?
10. Why did you come to Spain?
11. What time did you go to bed last Monday?
12. Did you have a shower yesterday?
13. Who did you see at the weekend?
14. Where did you speak Spanish yesterday?
15. What was the last book that you read?

16. PRETERITE IN CONTEXT- EL CUMPLEAÑOS DE CARMEN.

PRACTICE A: Practice reading this text out loud.

Ayer, día de mí cumpleaños, <u>me levanté</u> a las siete, como todos los días. Desayuné con mi marido en la casa y trabajé toda la mañana como siempre. Normalmente a mediodía vuelvo a casa para comer pero ayer comí en un restaurante, Mesón de Miguel, con mi marido Paco. Luego fuimos al Corte Inglés para comprar un regalo para mí y llegué un poco tarde a la oficina.
Cuando entré en mi despacho vi un pastel de cumpleaños grande en la mesa con dos botellas de champán. Todos mis compañeros cantaron "Cumpleaños Felíz" y me regalaron una pulsera en nombre de todos ellos. Estuve muy felíz..
Por la tarde visitamos a mis padres y cenamos con ellos. También vinieron mis hermanos y primos para cenar con nosotros. Pasé un día muy agradable.

VERB	INFINITIVE	ENGLISH	TENSE	PERSON
1. me levanté	levantarse	To get up	preterite	1st person singular
2.				
3.				
4.				
5.				
6.				
7.				
8.				
9.				
10.				
11.				
12.				
13.				
14.				
15.				
16.				
17.				
18.				
19.				

PRACTICE B: Pick out the 19 verbs and complete the verb identification table below as per the example.

PRACTICE C: Translate the text into English.

PRACTICE D: Translate these questions into Spanish and answer in Spanish.

1. What day was it yesterday?
2. What time did Carmen get up?
3. Who did she have breakfast with and where?
4. Where does she normally have lunch?
5. Where did she have lunch yesterday and with whom?
6. Where did they go then and why?
7. What did she see when she entered the office?
8. What did her workmates sing?
9. What did they give her as a present?
10. What did they do in the evening?
11. Who came to dinner also?
12. Did she have a nice day?

PRACTICE E: Write a short description of what you did on your last birthday. Use as much preterite as possible.

17. UNA TARDE INOLVIDABLE.

Yo trabajo en una compañía de seguros, soy oficinista. Paso cinco días a la semana, durante casi siete horas, sentado a una mesa. He trabajado allí durante catorce años.

Hace dos años, empecé a sentir depresiones. Fui al médico y me recomendó hacer ejercicio. Probé el tenis, pero lo encontré muy difícil. Me apunté a un gimnasio, pero me aburrí pronto. Las depresiones empeoraron.

Un día, un compañero de trabajo me invitó a ver un partido de fútbol entre el equipo local y otro de fuera. Fue una tarde inolvidable. Los espectadores gritaron sin parar para animar nuestro equipo. Insultaron al árbitro por algunos faltas contra los nuestros y saltaron de alegría con el gol que metimos. Ganamos. Tuvimos una fiesta grande. Lo pasamos muy bien.

Desde entonces, veo todos los partidos de mi equipo, en casa y fuera. Algunos fines de semana viajo hasta 1.500 kilómetros para animar a los nuestros. Soy el típico "hincha". El lunes por la mañana me levanto agotado, pero felíz. ¡Y se acabaron mis depresiones!

PRACTICE A: Practice reading this text out loud. Then find the 33 verbs and use them to complete the verb table below.

VERB	INFINITIVE	ENGLISH	TENSE	PERSON
1.				
2.				
3.				
4.				
5.				
6.				
7.				
8.				
9.				
10.				
11.				
12.				
13.				
14.				
15.				

16.				
17.				
18.				
19.				
20.				
21.				
22.				
23.				
24.				
25.				
26.				
27.				
28.				
29.				
30.				
31.				
32.				
33.				

PRACTICE B: Translate the text into English

PRACTICE C: Translate the questions below into Spanish and answer them in Spanish.

1. Where does he work and what does he do?
2. How does he spend the week?
3. How long has he worked there?
4. What happened two years ago?
5. What did the doctor recommend?
6. How did he find tennis?
7. Did he like the gym?
8. What happened one day?
9. What was the afternoon like?
10. What did the spectators do?
11. Did they win?
12. What does he do some weekends?
13. How does he wake up on a Monday morning?
14. Does he still have depression?

18. COMPARISON OF SER AND ESTAR-PRETERITE.

SER	TO BE	ESTAR
FUI	I WAS	ESTUVE
FUISTE	YOU WERE	ESTUVISTE
FUE	HE/SHE/IT WAS	ESTUVO
FUIMOS	WE WERE	ESTUVIMOS
FUISTEIS	YOU/S WERE	ESTUVISTEIS
FUERON	THEY WERE	ESTUVIERON

Remember that *"SER"* is used for- identity, nationality, origin, time, profession, possession, "natural" colours and intrinsic characteristics of people, places and things. *"ESTAR"* is used for **LOCATION** whether temporary or permanent, and temporary states and conditions of people, places or things, moods and emotions, "unnatural" colours and marital status.

The Preterite Tense is the past tense we use to talk about singular "one-off" actions in the past at a specific time. It normally translates to something we "did".

PRACTICE A: Translate the following sentences into Spanish using the appropriate form of "ser" or "estar".

1. The wedding was on Saturday.
2. The meal was in a restaurant in the centre of town. It was good.
3. At the wedding, the cutlery that was on the table was silver.
4. The exam was in the school, and it was very difficult.
5. In 1999 I was very young, and I was a student.
6. The last time that I was in London I had a terrible experience.
7. I was President of the club for one year.
8. Who was the winner yesterday?
9. It was a terrible party.
10. She was my best friend for ten years.

19. ALGO/NADA.

ALGO translates to the English **SOMETHING** or **ANYTHING**.
ALGO is used for **questions and positives** only.

Eg Is there **anything** to eat?- ¿Hay **ALGO** de comer?
     Yes, there is **something**- Si, hay **ALGO**

NADA also translates to **ANYTHING** or **NOTHING** but is only used for **negatives**.

E,g, Is there **anything** to drink?-¿Hay **ALGO** de beber?
     No, there isn´t **anything**- No, no hay **NADA**.

Examples:

Do you want **something**? ¿Quieres **ALGO**?
No, I don´t want **anything**. No, no quiero **NADA**.

Did he say **anything** yesterday? ¿Dijo **ALGO** ayer?
No, he didn´t say **anything**- No, no dijo **NADA**.

Have you done anything today?- ¿Has hecho **ALGO** hoy?
No, I haven´t done **anything**. No, no he hecho **NADA** hoy.

PRACTICE A: Translate these sentences into Spanish. Pay careful attention to the tense of the verb, which could be present, present perfect, or preterite.

1. Do you want something to eat?
   Yes, I want something.
   No, I do not want anything.

2. Do they know anything about Pedro?
   Yes they know something.
   No, they do not know anything.

3. Have they told you anything about the house?
   Yes, they have told me something.
   No, they have not told me anything.

4. Did you understand anything in Spanish?
   Yes, I understood something.
   No, I didn´t understand anything.

5. Are you going to buy something?
   Yes, I´m going to buy something.
   No, I´m not going to buy anything.

6. Have you seen anything?
   Yes, I have seen something.
   No, I haven´t seen anything.

7. Have you done anything this week?
   Yes, I´ve done something.
   No. I haven´t done anything.

8. Did you buy anything yesterday?
   Yes, I bought something.
   No, I didn´t buy anything.

9. Did he cook anything for you?
   Yes, he cooked something for me.
   No, he didn´t cook anything for me.

10. Did you make anything for him?
    Yes, I made something for him.
    No, I didn´t make anything for him.

11. Has she written anything?
    No, she hasn´t written anything.
    Yes, she has written something.

12. Did they break anything at the party?
    No, they didn`t break anything.
    Yes, they did break something.

13. Do you see anything?
    Yes, I see something.
    No, I don`t see anything.

14. Do you want anything?
    Yes, I want something.
    No, I don`t want anything.

15. Did you remember anything?
    Yes, I remembered something.
    No, I didn`t remember anything.

 Top Tips!!

6. Parts of the body- Los partes del cuerpo.

NB- generally parts of the body are not personalised.

E.g. Me lavo <u>las</u> manos **not** me lavo <u>mis</u> manos.

La mano- **hand**
El brazo- **arm**
El dedo- **finger**
La muñeca- **wrist**
La uña- **fingernail**
El codo- **elbow**
El hombro- **shoulder**
La espalda- **back**
El pecho- **chest**
La cadera- **hip**
La pierna- **leg**
La rodilla- **knee**
El tobillo- **ankle**
El pie- **foot**
La cara- **face**
Los ojos- **eyes**
La nariz- **nose**
La boca- **mouth**
La cabeza- **head**
El pelo- **hair**

20. ALGUIEN/NADIE

ALGUIEN translates to the English **SOMEONE** or **ANYONE**.
ALGUIEN is used for **questions and positives** only.

E. g. Is there anyone there?- ¿Hay **ALGUIEN** allí?
       Yes, there is someone- Si, hay **ALGUIEN**

NADIE translates to **ANYONE** or **NO-ONE** but is only used for **negatives.**

E. g. Is there anyone in the house? - ¿Hay **ALGUIEN** en la casa?
       No, no hay **NADIE**.

EXAMPLES:

Have you spoken to **ANYONE?** ¿Has hablado con **ALGUIEN**?

No I haven´t spoken to **ANYONE.** - No, no he hablado con **NADIE**

Do you know **ANYONE?**- ¿Conoces a **ALGUIEN**?

No, I don´t know **ANYONE.** - No, no conozco a **NADIE.**

PRACTICE A: Translate these sentences into Spanish. Again pay careful attention to the tense of the verb, which could be present, present perfect, or preterite.

1. Is there anyone in the restaurant?
   Yes, there is someone.
   No, there is not anyone.

2. Is he with anyone?
   Yes, he is with someone.
   No, he is not with anyone.

3. Have you seen anyone?
   Yes, I have seen someone.
   No, I have not seen anyone.

4. Are they going to the party with anyone?
   Yes, they are going to the party with someone.
   No, they are not going to the party with anyone.

5. Did you invite anyone?
   Yes, I invited someone.
   No, I did not invite anyone.

6. Have you(s) spoken to anyone?
   Yes, we have spoken to someone.
   No, we have not spoken to anyone.

7. Did anyone work there?
   Yes, someone worked there.
   No, no one worked there.

8. Did you speak to anyone in Spanish?
   Yes, I spoke to someone in Spanish.
   No, I did not speak to anyone in Spanish.

9. Do you like anyone?
   Yes, I like someone.
   No, I do not like anyone.

10. Did anyone come to the party?
    Yes, someone came.
    No, nobody came.

11. Have you kissed anyone?
    Yes, I have kissed someone.
    No, I have not kissed anyone.

12. Do you love anyone?
    Yes, I love someone.
    No, I do not love anyone.

13. Did you dance with anyone?
    Yes, I danced with someone.
    No, I did not dance with anyone.

14. Has he killed anyone?
    No, he has not killed anyone.
    Yes, he has killed someone.

15. Do you need someone?
    Yes, I need someone.
    No, I do not need anyone.

16. Has anyone done it for you?
    Yes, someone has done it for me.
    No, no one has done it for me.

Top Tips!!

7. The verb "doler"- to hurt.

"Doler" works in the same way as "gustar" (Level 1 chapter 26). It is a dipthong verb (Level 1 chapter 22) in the present tense.

E.g. Me duelen **las manos**- My hands hurt.
   Me duele **la cabeza**- My head hurts.
   Le duelen **la piernas**- His/her legs hurt.
   Nos duele **la espalda**- Our backs hurt.
   ¿Te duele **algo?**- Do you hurt anywhere?
   Les duele la **naríz-** Their nose hurts.
   ¿Os duelen **los pies?-** Do your feet hurt?
   Me ha dolido **la espalda todo el día**- My back has hurt me all day.

To talk about a person or an action that has hurt you, use "hacer daño".

E.g. Me ha hecho mucho daño- He has hurt me a lot.
   Tu comportamiento le hace daño- Your behaviour hurts him/her.
   Perder su trabajo les hizo mucho daño- Losing their job hurt them a lot.

21. THE IMPERFECT TENSE.

The Imperfect tense is also known as the past continuous. One thing it has in common with the preterite is that it describes actions that are past and finished and have no relationship to the present. However, whereas the preterite describes singular, one off actions at a specific time and place, this tense is used to describe repeated past actions. It relates to things we "used" to do, and actions in the past that have no specific beginning or end, i.e. things that we "were doing".

The good news is that most verbs are regular in this tense!! To make it, we take off the "ar", "er" and "ir" endings of the verbs and add on individual endings to represent the grammatical persons.

Estudiar-to study
(used to study/
was studying)

estudi/**aba**
estudi/**abas**
estudi/**aba**
estudi/**ábamos**
estudi/**abais**
estudi/**aban**

Tener-to have
(used to have/
was having)

ten/**ía**
ten/**ías**
ten/**ía**
ten/**íamos**
ten/**íais**
ten/**ían**

Venir-to come
(used to come/
was coming)

ven/**ía**
ven/**ías**
ven/**ía**
ven/**íamos**
ven/**íais**
ven/**ían**

Note that the endings for "er" and "ir" verbs are the same.

There are only 3 irregular verbs in this tense:

"Ser": era, eras, era, éramos, erais, eran (used to be, was being)
"Ver": veía, veías, veía, veíamos, veíais, veían (used to see, was seeing)
"Ir": iba, ibas, iba, íbamos, ibais, iban (used to go, was going)

PRACTICE A: Translate the sentences below-they all use the imperfect tense.

1. We used to speak on the telephone every night.
2. The sun was shining.
3. When I was a child, I lived in England.
4. They were listening to the radio.

5. Where did you use to play when you were a child?
6. I was swimming in the sea.
7. She used to have a dog.
8. Their teacher used to shout all the time.
9. Where did you use to work?
10. Carmen used to clean the house at weekends.
11. They always used to get up at 7 o´clock (in order to) go to work.
12. I was getting dressed.
13. His father was an accountant.
14. I was watching my favourite programme on the television.
15. It was very sunny in Spain.

Top Tips!!

8. "Aunque".

"Aunque" is a handy word that can translate as follows:

1. Although.

E.g. Aunque estaba lloviznando, decidimos salir- Although it was drizzling, we decided to go out.

2. Even though.

E.g. Aunque era muy caro, lo compré- Even though it was very expensive, I bought it.

3. But.

E.g. Es inteligente aunque algo rara.
She is intelligent but a little strange.

20. THE IMPERFECT TENSE IN CONTEXT.

Cuando era niña, vivía en Manchester con mi familia. Tenía cuatro hermanos, dos hermanos y dos hermanas. Todos tenían más años que yo.

Iba a la escuela en mi barrio, y me gustaba mucho. Jugaba en las calles y en el campo. Entonces era más seguro para los niños y no habían tantos coches. Había un parque grande cerca de mi casa y me acuerdo muy bien de un año cuando hizo mucho frio y nevó mucho. Pudimos jugar en la nieve todos los días.

Siempre quería un perro, pero mis padres no me dejaban. Mi padre era estricto, pero simpático. Trabajaba en una oficina y nunca ganaba mucho dinero. Mi madre trabajaba en la casa. Los dos tenían bicicletas, nunca tenían coche.

Nunca teníamos mucho dinero, pero más o menos estábamos contentos.

PRACTICE A: Practice reading this text out loud.

PRACTICE B: Pick out the 25 verbs in the text and complete the verb identification table below as per the example.

VERB	INFINITIVE	ENGLISH	TENSE	PERSON
1. era	ser	To be	imperfect	1st person singular
2.				
3.				
4.				
5.				
6.				
7.				
8.				
9.				
10.				
11.				
12.				
13.				
14.				
15.				
16.				

17.				
18.				
19.				
20.				
21.				
22.				
23.				
24.				
25.				

PRACTICE C: Translate the text into English.

PRACTICE D: Translate and answer the questions in Spanish.

1. Where did she live when she was a child?
2. How many brothers and sisters did she have?
3. Were they younger than her?
4. Where did she go to school?
5. Where did she use to play?
6. What does she remember very well?
7. When could they play in the snow?
8. What did she always want?
9. What was her father like?
10. Where did he work?
11. Where did her mother work?
12. Were they happy?

PRACTICE E: Now write about your childhood. Use a combination of past tenses.

23. IMPERFECT TENSE- CONVERSATION PRACTICE.

PRACTICE A: Translate these questions into Spanish and answer in Spanish. Practice them with a friend if possible.

1. Where did you use to live in the UK?
2. Where did you go to school?
3. Where did you use to play?
4. What time did you use to get up when you were working?
5. What did you used to do on Sundays?
6. Where did you use to buy your clothes?
7. What did you use to put on in the winter?
8. What did you use to watch on the television on Saturday nights?
9. Did you eat in restaurants often?
10. Did you play any sports?
11. When did you use to go on holiday?
12. Why did you want to come to Spain?
13. Could you speak Spanish before coming here?
14. When you were a child did you know how to swim?
15. Where was your first house?
16. What colour was your first car?
17. Did you always do your homework?
18. Did you behave well at school?
19. When you were a child did you have any animals?
20. What did you want to be?

24. COMPARISON OF SER AND ESTAR-IMPERFECT TENSE.

SER	TO BE	ESTAR
ERA	I WAS	ESTABA
ERAS	YOU WERE	ESTABAS
ERA	HE/SHE/IT WAS	ESTABA
ÉRAMOS	WE WERE	ESTÁBAMOS
ERAIS	YOU/S WERE	ESTABAIS
ERAN	THEY WERE	ESTABAN

PRACTICE A: Refer to Chapter 16 for the explanation of the difference between "ser" and "estar" and translate the following sentences into Spanish

1. What was Carlos´s father like?
2. Where were you? I was looking for you.
3. She was an actress that I liked very much.
4. My old house was in the centre of town.
5. They were always in a good mood and used to tell us funny stories.
6. I was ill and could not go to the party.
7. I wanted to buy the shoes but they were very expensive.
8. Why was he in that car?
9. Juan was very tall and handsome.
10. When he was in Spain, he was a policeman.

PRACTICE B: Translate.

1. (a) Every Monday she was ill and couldn't work.
   (b) Every Monday the queues were long.

2. (a) On Fridays I was at work until 8 o´clock.
   (b) On Fridays the drinks were cheap.

3. (a) Every week I was there at his house.
   (b) Every week they were more expensive.

4. (a) When I was a child I was always playing in the park.
   (b) When I was a child I was always in the park.

5. (a) She was always tall for her age.
   (b) The shops were always closed on Sundays.

6. (a) They never were very good dancers.
   (b) You(s) were never here when I needed you/s

7. (a) I was never strict.
   (b) They were never in class.

8. (a) I used to be a singer in a bar.
   (b) He was always happy when she was there.

9. (a) You(s) were always very intelligent.
   (b) You(s) were often on the beach when I was there.

10. (a) Every year the holidays were more and more expensive.
    (b) Every year they were open later.

Top Tips!!

> 9. "Soler".
>
> "Soler" is another one of those handy verbs that can be used to make life easier when speaking Spanish. We use it to express things we normally do, usually do or used to do, followed by the infinitive of the other verb. It is a dipthong verb (Level 1 chapter 22) in the present tense.
>
> E.g. Suelo ir a la playa los domingos- I usually go to the beach on Sundays.
> Suelo comer a las dos- I normally have lunch at 2 o´clock.
>
> To talk of things we used to do, we put "soler" in the imperfect tense.
>
> E.g. Solíamos comprar muchos zapatos- We used to buy a lot of shoes.
> Solían hablar pero ahora no- They used to talk but not now.

25. VERB PRACTICE.

PRACTICE A: Write the verb forms of these verbs in the spaces provided. Do it in pencil so you can go back at a later date and test yourself by doing it again. Try to do it first as far as possible without looking them up, then check your answers.

1. HABLAR

PRESENT	P. PERFECT	PRETERITE	IMPERFECT

2. PONER

PRESENT	P. PERFECT	PRETERITE	IMPERFECT

3. ESTAR

PRESENT	P. PERFECT	PRETERITE	IMPERFECT

4. SER

PRESENT	P. PERFECT	PRETERITE	IMPERFECT

5. LEER

PRESENT	P. PERFECT	PRETERITE	IMPERFECT

6. SUBIR

PRESENT	P. PERFECT	PRETERITE	IMPERFECT

7. VOLVER

PRESENT	P. PERFECT	PRETERITE	IMPERFECT

8. IR

PRESENT	P. PERFECT	PRETERITE	IMPERFECT

9. CANTAR

PRESENT	P. PERFECT	PRETERITE	IMPERFECT

10. QUERER

PRESENT	P. PERFECT	PRETERITE	IMPERFECT

11. PODER

PRESENT	P. PERFECT	PRETERITE	IMPERFECT

12. TENER

PRESENT	P. PERFECT	PRETERITE	IMPERFECT

13. MIRAR

PRESENT	P. PERFECT	PRETERITE	IMPERFECT

14. ABRIR

PRESENT	P. PERFECT	PRETERITE	IMPERFECT

15. LEVANTARSE

PRESENT	P. PERFECT	PRETERITE	IMPERFECT

16. ACOSTARSE

PRESENT	P. PERFECT	PRETERITE	IMPERFECT

17. DECIR

PRESENT	P. PERFECT	PRETERITE	IMPERFECT

18. VENIR

PRESENT	P. PERFECT	PRETERITE	IMPERFECT

19. LLEVAR

PRESENT	P. PERFECT	PRETERITE	IMPERFECT

20. PENSAR

PRESENT	P. PERFECT	PRETERITE	IMPERFECT

26. COMPARISON OF TENSES.

PRACTICE A: Translate these questions into Spanish and answer in Spanish. Each verb has one question in each of the tenses we have covered: the present simple, the present perfect, the preterite and the imperfect. Try practicing asking and answering them with a friend.

1. **HACER**

   What do you do on Saturdays?
   What have you done today?
   What did you do last Saturday?
   What were you doing on Saturday morning?

2. **LEVANTARSE**

   What time do you normally get up?
   What time did you get up yesterday?
   What time did you used to get up?
   What time did you get up this morning?

3. **IR**

   Where do you go shopping?
   Where have you been today?
   Where did you go the day before yesterday?
   Where did you use to go on Sundays?

4. **HABLAR**

   How many languages do you speak?
   Who have you spoken to today?
   Did you speak to anyone on the telephone last night?
   Were you speaking to anyone on the telephone on Sunday?

5. **PONER/COMPRAR**

   Where do you put your keys?
   Where have you put your dictionary?
   Where did you put the last thing that you bought?
   Where did you used to put your clothes?

6. **ESCRIBIR**

   Do you write many emails?
   Have you written anything for a magazine?
   Did you write to your family last week?
   Did you used to write many letters before the internet?

7. **ESTAR**

   Where were you on Sunday?
   Were you often at the cinema in Britain?
   Have you ever been to Mexico?
   Where are you?

8. **SER**

   Have you ever been a student?
   Where are you from?
   How was your last birthday?
   Where was your last Spanish teacher from?

9. **BEBER**

   What did you drink last night before dinner?
   What do you drink in the morning?
   What did you used to drink in a restaurant?
   Have you drunk coffee today?

10. **ESTUDIAR**

    What do you study?
    Have you studied a lot this month?
    What did you study last year?
    Where were you studying last year?

Top Tips!!

10. "Parecer".

Another handy verb that operates in the same way as "gustar" (Level 1 chapter 26) is "parecer". It´s literal meaning is "to seem" or "appear" but it can translate to "think".

E.g. Me parece estupendo- I think it´s great. (Literally "it seems great to me".)

¿No os parece buen idea?- Don´t you(s) think it is a good idea? (Literally "Doesn´t it seem like a good idea to you(s)?")

Los vecinos siempre nos parecían muy simpáticos- We always thought that the neighbours were very nice. (Literally the neighbours always seemed very nice to us.)

Nunca les parecía una casa bonita- They never thought it was a pretty house. (Literally "It never seemed like a pretty house to them".)

27. IDIOMATIC EXPRESSIONS.

PRACTICE A: Match up the expressions.

1. ver con malos ojos	1. to not be my cup of tea
2. no ser plato de mi gusto	2. to skip a class
3. fumarse una clase	3. to be lucky
4. dar mala espina	4. to be a dirty old man
5. beber como una esponja	5. to carry the can
6. tener buena estrella	6. to take a dim view
7. andar con cien ojos	7. to make one suspicious
8. estar en la edad del pavo	8. to lose the plot
9. pagar el pato	9. to rain cats and dogs
10. estar de uñas (con alguien)	10. to keep your eyes open
11. tener un humor de perros	11. to be a bit dim
12. ser un viejo verde	12. to be at daggers drawn
13. ser de pasta dura	13. to be in a bad mood
14. perder los papeles	14. to be tough as old boots
15. no tener luces	15. to be at a difficult age
16. llover a cántaros	16. to drink like a fish

PRACTICE B: Use them to translate these sentences in the appropriate tense.

1. Juan´s brother drinks like a fish.
2. It was raining cats and dogs whilst we were in Galicia.
3. Carmen was a person who always took a dim view of everything.
4. Maria´s son is 14. He is at a difficult age.
5. I am always carrying the can for him.
6. When they were children they were always at daggers drawn.
7. When Pedro woke up last Sunday he was in a foul mood.
8. I think that she has lost the plot.
9. Uncle Frank was always a dirty old man.
10. She has recovered. She is as tough as old boots.
11. He is good looking enough, but he is not my cup of tea.
12. We didn´t feel like studying yesterday so we skipped a class.
13. He couldn´t understand what I said because he is a bit dim.
14. They won the lottery last week. They have always been lucky.
15. I always kept my eyes wide open when he was around, he made me feel suspicious.

28. LA ACTRIZ ESTRELLA FUGAZ.

Cuando **era** pequeña vivía en el campo. Una noche de verano su padre la llevó a dar un paseo. De repente, una estrella cruzó el cielo de un lado a otro. Fue una estrella fugaz. Aquello le impresionó mucho, y, por eso. cuando empezó a trabajar en el cine, decidió llamarse "Estrella Fugaz".

Actualmente Estrella es una de las mujeres más ricas y famosas del mundo, pero dice que para ella, el dinero no es importante. Son más importantes su carrera , su perrita "Luz" y el amor.

Aunque es rica y bella, sigue soltera. Siempre ha sido afortunada pero es muy inconstante en el amor. Se enamora fácilmente y deja de amar con la misma facilidad.

Llevó a su abuela de sesenta años al estreno de su última película. En cuanto empezó la película la abuela se durmió y no se despertó hasta el final.
Le preguntó Estrella: "Abuela, ¿no te gusta mi película?"
La abuela sonrió y dijo: "Para verte hacer tonterías, no necesito venir al cine".

Estrella dice que su abuela es una de las mujeres más inteligentes que ha conocido, y que cuando su abuela era joven se parecía mucho a ella.

PRACTICE A: Practice reading this out loud. Then pick out the 39 verbs in this text and use them to complete the verb identification table below as per the example.

VERB	INFINITIVE	ENGLISH	TENSE	PERSON
1. era	ser	To be	imperfect	3rd p.sing.
2.				
3.				
4.				
5.				
6.				
7.				
8.				
9.				
10.				
11.				
12.				

13.				
14.				
15.				
16.				
17.				
18.				
19.				
20.				
21.				
22.				
23.				
24.				
25.				
26.				
27.				
28.				
29.				
30.				
31.				
32.				
33.				
34.				
35.				
36.				
37.				
38.				
39.				

PRACTICE B: Translate into English.

PRACTICE C: Translate the questions into Spanish and answer in Spanish.

1. Where did Estrella live when she was small?
2. Where did her father take her one night?
3. What happened suddenly?
4. What did she decide to call herself when she started work in the cinema?
5. What is she like?
6. Is money important?

7. Is she married?
8. Who did she take to the first night of her latest film?
9. What did she do as soon as the film started?
10. When did she wake up?
11. What did her grandmother say when she asked her if she liked the film?
12. What does Estrella say about her grandmother?

29. THE PAST PERFECT (PLUPERFECT OR "PLUSCAMPERFECTO")

The pastperfect is a compound tense the same as the **PRESENT PERFECT**. In other words, it is formed by 2 separate verbs rather than one. It translates to the English as to "**HAD** done something". Sometimes referred to as "the past of the past", we use this tense to describe actions in the past that took place before another past action. E.g. When I arrived, you **had already left.**

As with the **PRESENT PERFECT**, We don't use the verb **"tener"** that normally means "to have" to construct the first part. We use the helper or auxiliary verb **"haber"** that is used to specifically to construct tenses. To make the **PAST PERFECT**, we conjugate it in the imperfect tense as follows:

Había- I had/ I'd
Habías- you had/ you'd
Había- he/she/it had- He'd/she'd/it'd
Habíamos- we had/ we'd
Habíais- you had/ you'd
Habían- they had/they'd

The second part is formed using the **past participle** of the second verb, i.e the action that we "had done". This is identical to how we made them when we learnt the **PRESENT PERFECT**. Regular **past participles** are formed as follows:

"Ar" verbs- remove the "ar" and add "ado". E.g hablado- spoken
"Er" verbs- remove the "er" and add "ido". E.g aprendido-learnt
"Ir" verbs-same as "er" verbs. E.g vivido-lived

Just like in English, **IRREGULAR** past participles have no pattern and simply have to be learnt.

PRACTICE A: Here are a group of verbs that have irregular participles. What is the English participle for each verb? The first one has been done for you.

1. Escribir - to write   - escrito -   written.
2. Hacer –   - hecho -
3. Romper –   - roto -
4. Ver -   - visto –

5. Volver -   - vuelto -
6. Decir -   - dicho -
7. Abrir -   - abierto -
8. Morir -   - muerto -
9. Poner -   - puesto -
10. Cubrir -   - cubierto -
11. Freir -   - frito -

PRACTICE B: Translate.

1. I had already cleaned the car when it started to rain.
2. When we arrived home he hadn´t done anything.
3. When they returned home all the flowers had died.
4. I had put the money in the drawer and then someone called at the door.
5. He had called her at least ten times before leaving.
6. I couldn´t install the programme because the shop hadn´t given me enough information.
7. The thieves had broken all the doors and the windows.
8. When I went to work at seven they still hadn´t found the keys to get in.
9. We had opened all the windows because it was hot.
10. I didn´t want to go to the cinema because I had already seen the fim.
11. When I saw him he hadn´t said anything to Carmen.
12. They had written twenty emails before receiving a reply.
13. I had paid for the vase, then I dropped it and broke it.
14. We had lived in many other countries before coming to Spain.
15. Even the day before they still hadn't received the invitation.
16. She had never seen him before the day of their wedding.
17. I wasn´t nervous because I had practised the speech for 2 hours the night before.
18. Had you cleaned the house before the party?
19. You(s) hadn´t turned off the lights before leaving the office last night.
20. They hadn´t done anything all week.

PRACTICE C: Translate into Spanish.

We had never been in France before although we had travelled a lot in the rest of Europe. My husband had always wanted to go to Paris and he had won quite a lot of money on the lottery, so we decided to go and stay in a four star hotel in the centre of the City. Before leaving, we had bought new suitcases, lots of clothes and two pairs of expensive sunglasses. We had also bought an Ipad so we could take lots of photos, and we had asked our neighbours to look after our two cats. The day we left for the airport the sun was shining and we were happy that we had prepared everything and could relax and enjoy our holiday.

30. SUMMARY OF PAST TENSES

1. THE PRESENT PERFECT.

Compound tense-straddles 2 time zones-translates to "to have done" something.

Formation:

A. To have (use "haber", not "tener")

he - I have
has - You have
ha – He/she/it has
hemos- We have
habéis- You(s) have
han- They have

B. Past participle of the second verb, i.e the action that we "have done". Regular **past participles**:

"Ar" verbs- remove the "ar" and add "ado", i.e **hablado- spoken**
"Er" verbs- remove the "er" and add "ido", i.e **aprendido-learnt**
"Ir" verbs-same as "er" verbs, i.e **vivido-lived**

B. Irregular participles. What is the English participle for each verb? The first one has been done for you.
escribir- escrito, hacer- hecho, romper-roto, ver- visto, volver- vuelto, decir- dicho, abrir- abierto, morir- muerto, poner- puesto, cubrir- cubierto, freir- frito.

2. THE PAST PERFECT.

Translates to "had" done something.

Formation: Also compound tense.
A: Use past tense of "haber"

Había- I had   **habíamos-** we had
Habías- you had   **habíais-** you(s) had
Había- he/she/it had **habían-** they had

B: Past Participle as "Present Perfect" above.

3. THE PRETERITE.

Singular completed actions in the past, at a specific point in time. In English, anything we 'did'.

Regular verbs:

"Ar"- é, aste, ó, amos, asteis, aron
"Er/ ir"- í, iste, ió, imos, isteis, ieron

Irregular verbs:

* hacer- hic	tener -tuv
poner- pus	*decir - dij
poder-pud	*conducir- conduj
saber -sup	*traer - traj
estar - estuv	querer - quis
* dar - d	venir- vin

Endings – e, iste, o, imos, isteis, ieron (except dar-takes the endings for REGULAR "er" verbs

"Ser"/ "Ir"- fui, fuiste, fue, fuimos, fuisteis, fueron.

4. THE IMPERFECT.

Past repeated actions or actions with no specific beginning or end- background descriptions in the past-things we "were doing" or "used to do". Most verbs are regular in this tense.

<u>Regular verbs</u>
"Ar"- aba, abas, aba, ábamos, abais, aban
"Er"/ "ir" - ía, ías, ía, íamos, íais, ían

There are only 3 irregular verbs in this tense:

"Ser": era, eras, era, éramos, erais, eran
"Ver": veía, veías, veía, veíamos, veíais, veían
"Ir": iba, ibas, iba, íbamos, ibais, iban

31. COMPARISON OF TENSES ENGLISH TO SPANISH 1.

Yesterday evening we left the beach at about half past six and returned to the hotel in our car. Our hotel was in the village about 5 kilometres from the beach and our friend's hotel was two kilometres further on. On our way to the village we saw an old fisherman, he was walking slowly along the road. He was about seventy and was carrying a large box in his hand. We stopped the car and asked him where he was going. He explained to us that he had found the box in the sand near his fishing boat. When he opened it he found some papers and also an envelope with thousands of euros. Now he was going to the police station in the village. He got into the car and we took him to the police station where he gave everything to the police.

PRACTICE A: Find the 19 verbs in this text and use them to fill in the verb identification table below like the example given.

VERB	INFINITIVE	SPANISH	TENSE	PERSON
1. we left	To leave	salir	preterite	1st plural
2.				
3.				
4.				
5.				
6.				
7.				
8.				
9.				
10.				
11.				
12.				
13.				
14.				
15.				
16.				
17.				
18.				
19.				

PRACTICE B: Translate the text into Spanish.

PRACTICE C: Translate these questions into Spanish and answer in Spanish.

1. When did they leave the beach?
2. How did they return to the hotel?
3. Where was their hotel?
4. Where was their friend's hotel?
5. What did they see on the way to the village?
6. How old was he?
7. What was he carrying in his hand?
8. What did they do then?
9. Where had he found the box?
10. What did he find when he opened it?
11. What was he doing now?
12. Where did they take him?
13. What did he do there?
14. Have you ever found anything unusual?
15. What did you do?

32. COMPARISON OF TENSES ENGLISH TO SPANISH 2.

When **we were** in Spain last year we spent a night in a small town in the mountains close to Madrid. Scarcely had we arrived when the owner of the hotel where we were going to stay told us that the following day the cyclists in the tour of Spain were going to pass through the village.

I had seen the race before but my friends were very interested and so we all got up very early in order to see it. However, when we arrived at the main square, we found a huge crowd already waiting for the arrival of the cyclists. We waited a long time but there was a lot of excitement when at last the leaders appeared.

Soon they had all gone and everyone went to the cafés to talk about what they had seen. Nothing sensational had happened but everybody seemed to be very animated. In the evening we watched a special television programme and we saw the cyclists pass through the main square on their way to Madrid. We saw ourselves too!!

PRACTICE A: Pick out the 29 verbs and use them to complete the verb recognition table below according to the example.

Verb in context	Infinitive	Spanish	Tense	Person
1. we were	To be	estar	preterite	1st p.plural
2.				
3.				
4.				
5.				
6.				
7.				
8.				
9.				
10.				
11.				
12.				
13.				
14.				
15.				
16.				

17.				
18.				
19.				
20.				
21.				
22.				
23.				
24.				
25.				
26.				
27.				
28.				
29.				

PRACTICE B: *Translate the text into Spanish.*

PRACTICE C: *Translate the questions and answer in Spanish.*

1. When were they in Spain?
2. Where did they spend one night?
3. What did the owner of the hotel where they were going to stay tell them?
4. Who had seen the race before?
5. What did they do in order to see it?
6. What did they find when they arrived at the main square?
7. Did they have to wait long?
8. What did everyone do after they had all gone?
9. How was everybody?
10. What did they watch that evening?
11. Who did they see also?
12. Have you ever seen a famous event? Write about it.

33. PRACTICE OF PAST TENSES, "ADIÓS MARÍA".

María García estudiaba intensamente la carrera de piano. Durante el día asistía el Conservatorio y por la noche, después de cenar, practicaba en casa en su piano particular. Con frecuencia María practicaba hasta la una o las dos de la madrugada. Esto molestaba a los vecinos. Algunos no podían dormir y se indignaban. Los vecinos, además, tenían mucha antipatía a su madre, Carmen. Carmen García era de familia noble y se consideraba superior a todos los demás habitantes de la calle. Era una señora muy orgullosa.

Llegó el verano y por la noche todos los vecinos abrían las ventanas para combatir el calor. Pero entonces oían el piano de María con más fuerza. Los vecinos gritaban- "Queremos dormir!! No hay derecho!! Esto es un abuso!!".
María aprobó sus exámenes con la máxima nota y le concedieron una beca para ampliar sus estudios en Viena. La noche antes de partir para aquella ciudad, la madre y su hija dieron una fiesta de despedida a sus familiares y amigos.

A la vez, todos los vecinos de la calle celebraron con una cena grande. Bebieron mucho champán y bailaron. La diversión duró hasta el amanecer y los vecinos bailaban, cantaban y aplaudían. Al final, gritaban todos "Adiós María, adiós!!!"

PRACTICE A: Underline the 33 verbs and use them to complete this verb recognition table.

VERB	INFINITIVE	ENGLISH	TENSE	PERSON
1.				
2.				
3.				
4.				
5.				
6.				
7.				
8.				
9.				
10.				
11.				
12.				
13.				
14.				

15.				
16.				
17.				
18.				
19.				
20.				
21.				
22.				
23.				
24.				
25.				
26.				
27.				
28.				
29.				
30.				
31.				
32.				
33.				

PRACTICE B. Translate the text into English.

PRACTICE C. Translate these questions into Spanish and answer them in Spanish.

1. What was María studying?
2. What did she used to do in the day?
3. What did she used to do after dinner?
4. Until what time did she often practice ?
5. Why did this bother the neighbours?
6. Why did the neighbours not like Maria´s mother, Carmen?
7. What was she like?
8. What happened when summer arrived?
9. Why were the neighbours shouting?
10. Did Maria pass her exams?
11. Where was she going to study?
12. What did Maria and her mother do the night before leaving?
13. What did the neighbours do at the same time?
14. Until what time did the fun last?
15. What were the neighbours doing?
16. What were they shouting at the end?

34. TRANSLATION FROM ENGLISH TO SPANISH- MIXED TENSES.

A few weeks ago, I went on holiday to Spain. First, I went to Barcelona where I was for 3 days. I visited all the interesting places. The hotel was near "Las Ramblas" and was very comfortable. It was a bit cloudy, but it did not rain. I met many nice people there and I have never seen such beautiful buildings.

After Barcelona, I visited Palma de Mallorca. I went by boat and I stayed there for ten days. I did not like it very much as there were a lot of tourists and the apartment was very noisy. The weather was very bad also. However, now I have seen it but I do not want to return.

From Palma, I travelled by aeroplane to Valencia. I was there only two days. The hotel was very uncomfortable, and I had very little time to see the City. I have always wanted to visit the Science Museum, but I did not have time.

I caught the train to Madrid and was there for seven days. Although it rained for four days I had a great time. I went to the El Prado Museum, the Bernabeu Football Stadium, The Retiro Park and lots of other places, but it was very expensive. I have never paid so much money for a cup of coffee.

Then I went to Granada by coach. It was the prettiest place I have ever visited. I was there 6 days, the weather was great, and I met up with some friends that live there. We went to the Alhambra Palace, it was breath-taking. The city was very pretty, and the people were friendly. We went to see a Flamenco show and we skied on the Sierra Nevada. The snow was very pretty.

Finally, I went to Salamanca by car where I did an Intensive Course in Spanish. I have never studied a foreign language before, and I found it difficult but interesting. The teachers were very nice, also the other students. I made a lot of friends and after 15 days I returned home. I have had a fantastic experience.

BREAK THE LANGUAGE BARRIER LEVEL 2
WWW.ELPRINCIPECENTRE.ORG
info@elprincipecentre.org

PRACTICE A: Pick out the 58 verbs in this text and fill out the identification box below. The first three have been done for you.

VERB	INFINITIVE	SPANISH	TENSE	PERSON
1. I went	To go	ir	preterite	1st p.singular
2. I went	To go	ir	preterite	1st p.singular
3. I was	To be	estar	preterite	1st p.singular
4.				
5.				
6.				
7.				
8.				
9.				
10.				
11.				
12.				
13.				
14.				
15.				
16.				
17.				
18.				
19.				
20.				
21.				
22.				
23.				
24.				
25.				
26.				
27.				
28.				
29.				
30.				
31.				
32.				
33.				

Copyright© Vicki Marie Riley 1999-2023. All rights reserved.

34.				
35.				
36.				
37.				
38.				
39.				
40.				
41.				
42.				
43.				
44.				
45.				
46.				
47.				
48.				
49.				
50.				
51.				
52.				
53.				
54.				
55.				
56.				
57.				
58.				

PRACTICE B: Translate the text into Spanish.

PRACTICE C: Translate these questions into Spanish and answer in Spanish.

1. When did she go on holiday?
2. Where did she go first?
3. How long was she there?
4. What was the hotel like?
5. What was the weather like?
6. Who did she meet?
7. What has she never seen?
8. Where did she go then?
9. How did she go there?

10. How long was she there?
11. Did she like it?
12. Why?
13. Where did she go then and how?
14. What has she always wanted to visit?
15. How did she get to Madrid?
16. Did she have a good time?
17. How long was she in Granada?
18. What was the Alhambra Palace like?
19. What did they do on the Sierra Nevada?
20. How did she get to Salamanca?
21. What did she do there?
22. Has she had a good experience?

 Top Tips!!

---

11. Ponerse.

We have seen that "ponerse" the reflexive form of "poner" (to put) translates to "put on" as in clothes etc. However, it can also translate to "to get" or "become" as in "get nervous" or other emotional states.

E,g. Siempre me pongo enfermo los lunes- I always get (feel) ill on Mondays.

El sábado pasado fui a la entrevista y me puse muy nervioso- Last Friday I went to the interview and I got/became very anxious.

Nos poníamos muy tristes- We got/became very sad.

¿Por qué te pusiste tan enfadado ayer?- Why did you get/become so angry yesterday?

Se pusieron muy felices en el día de su boda- they got/became very happy on their wedding day.

35. POSTSCRIPT.

I hope you have enjoyed this book and that your Spanish has improved accordingly. Go over the excercises on a regular basis and practise speaking and listening as often as possible. Repetition and practice is essential for fluidity and confidence with your Spanish, but remember not to be too hard on yourself and expect immediate perfection. You will get it wrong many times before you get it right!!

Keep up the practice as much as possible. Listen to Spanish radio, watch the Spanish TV, go to the Spanish cinema and change the language on your Netflix.

When you are confident with all the components of this Level 2 course you should be communicating effectively in Spanish in the past tenses and ready to move on to Level 3.

Don't forget the YouTube channel, where you will find the audio of all the exercises. The link is below, the videos are numbered, and the page numbers are in the description. Please give a thumbs up if you find the video useful, and subscribe for updates (this is FREE, no cost involved).

You will also find all social media links and contact details.

Lastly, if you have the time and feel so inclined, please leave a review on Amazon of this book and how it has helped you to learn Spanish. Thank you ☺

Happy practising!!!

Vicki

Facebook: https://www.facebook.com/easyspanishandenglishwithvicki/
Instagram: https://www.instagram.com/easyspanishandenglishwithvicki/
Twitter: @esayspanishandenglishwithvicki
YouTube: https://www.youtube.com/channel/UCm38MRBMVXrV6JblhmQ7xOg
Blog: Confessions of a Spanish teacher:
https://confessionsofaspanishteacher.wordpress.com/

36. KEY TO "TOP TIPS".

	PAGE NUMBER
1. PLACEMENT OF REFLEXIVE PRONOUNS	9
2. "QUEDAR/ SE"	9
3. LETTER/ EMAIL ENDINGS	17
4. "SABER" AND "CONOCER"	20
5. "SALIR" AND "DEJAR"	23
6. PARTS OF THE BODY	45
7. "DOLER"	48
8. "AUNQUE"	50
9. "SOLER"	55
10. "PARECER"	64
11. "PONERSE"	83

37. ANSWERS.

1. INTRODUCE YOURSELF.

PRACTICE A: The answers are free but the correct verb form is given.

1. ¿Cómo te llamas? Me llamo ....
2. ¿Dónde vives? Vivo ......
3. ¿Vives en una casa o un apartamento/piso? Vivo.....
4. ¿Cómo es tu casa? Mi casa es ....
5. ¿Estás casado? No/estoy......
6. ¿Tienes niños? No /tengo.....
7. ¿Cuántos años tienen? Tengo.....
8. ¿Dónde viven? Viven......
9. ¿Qué haces en tu tiempo libre? Free answer.
10. ¿Cuántos idiomas hablas? Hablo.....
11. ¿Por qué es el español importante para tí? Para mí, es importante.....
12. ¿Cuándo es tu cumpleaños? Mi cumpleaños es ......
13. ¿Por qué quieres aprender español? Quiero aprender español...........
14. ¿Dónde trabajas? No /trabajo............
15. ¿Qué te gusta más de España? Me gusta/n más..........
16. ¿Qué te gusta menos? Me gusta/n menos.............
17. ¿Te gusta la comida española? Si/No/ me gusta
18. ¿Comprendes los verbos españoles? Comprendo......
19. ¿Por qué debes comer (las) verduras? Debo comer (las) verduras ....
20. ¿A quién recuerdas más de la escuela? Recuerdo más a ....
21. ¿Dónde quieres ir de vacaciones? Quiero ir a ....
22. ¿Dónde está tu coche? Mí coche está.........
23. ¿Quién es tu mejor amigo? Mí mejor amigo es.............
24. ¿Adónde vas normalmente los domingos? Normalmente voy......
25. ¿De dónde eres? Soy de ....
26. ¿Estás feliz/contento/a? Si/ No /estoy.........
27. ¿Cómo eres? Soy.......
28. ¿Qué haces por la tarde/noche? Free answer.
29. ¿Qué bebes en un restaurante? Bebo........
30. ¿Bebes mucho café? Si/No bebo.......

2. REFLEXIVE VERBS

PRACTICE A:

1. Levantarse-
To get up.

Me	levanto
Te	levantas
Se	levanta
Nos	levantamos
Os	levantáis
Se	levantan

2. Despertarse-
(dipthong **e** to **ie**)
To wake up.

Me	despierto
Te	despiertas
Se	despierta
Nos	despertamos
Os	despertáis
Se	despiertan

3. Pintarse -
To put on make-up, paint one´s nails

Me	pinto
Te	pintas
Se	pinta
Nos	pintamos
Os	pintáis
Se	pintan

4. Lavarse -
To have a wash/
wash oneself.

Me	lavo
Te	lavas
Se	lava
Nos	lavamos
Os	laváis
Se	lavan

5. Ducharse -

To have a shower/
shower oneself.

Me	ducho
Te	duchas
Se	ducha
Nos	duchamos
Os	ducháis
Se	duchan

6. Acostarse -
(dipthong **o**
to **ue**)
To go to bed.

Me	acuesto
Te	acuestas
Se	acuesta
Nos	acostamos
Os	acostáis
Se	acuestan

7. Afeitarse -
To have a shave,
shave oneself.

Me	afeito
Te	afeitas
Se	afeita
Nos	afeitamos
Os	afeitáis
Se	afeitan

8. Vestirse-
(dipthong **e** to **i**)
To get dressed

Me	visto
Te	vistes
Se	viste
Nos	vestimos
Os	vestís
Se	visten

9. Ponerse -
To put on, to get/
become.

Me	pongo
Te	pones
Se	pone
Nos	ponemos
Os	ponéis
Se	ponen

10. Peinarse –
To comb/
do one´s hair

Me	peino
Te	peinas
Se	peina
Nos	peinamos
Os	peináis
Se	peinan

PRACTICE B:

Verb	Infinitive	English Meaning	Meaning in context
1. me llamo	llamarse	To call oneself	I call myself
2. me levanto	levantarse	To get up	I get up
3. me ducho	ducharse	To have a shower	I have a shower
4. me afeito	afeitarse	To have a shave	I shave
5. me peino	peinarse	To comb/do one´s hair	I comb/do my hair
6. me visto	vestirse	To get dressed	I get dressed
7. se despierta	despertarse	To wake up	He wakes up
8. se queda	quedarse	To stay	He stays
9. se levantan	levantarse	To get up	They get up
10. se va	irse	To go (off)	She goes (off)
11. nos reuinimos	reunirse	To get together	We get together
12. nos acostamos	acostarse	To go to bed	We go to bed

PRACTICE C:

My name is Pedro Martinez and I am a mechanic. Every day, I get up at 7 o´clock. I go to the bathroom, I shower, I shave, and I do/comb my hair. Then I return to my room and I get dressed.

My brother sleeps in the same room. He almost always wakes up later. He is very lazy. Sometimes he stays in bed until 10 o´clock. He doesn´t work. He goes to the High School where he studies but sometimes he stays in bed because the classes are boring.

My parents also get up at 7. My mother prepares the breakfast and my father reads the paper. At 7.30 we have breakfast and then we leave the house. My father goes to the office, I go to the garage, my brother to the High School, and my mother goes (off) shopping.

At night we all get together again. We have dinner, we watch the television, and later we go to bed.

PRACTICE D:

1. ¿A qué hora se levanta Pedro? Pedro se levanta a las siete.
2. ¿Qué hace en el cuarto de baño? Se ducha, se afeita, y se peina.
3. ¿Qué hace cuando vuelve a su dormitorio? Se viste.
4. ¿Quién duerme en la misma habitación? Su hermano duerme en la misma habitación.
5. ¿Trabaja su hermano? No, no trabaja.
6. ¿Por qué a veces se queda en la cama? A veces se queda en cama porque las clases son aburridas.
7. ¿Quiénes también se levantan a las siete? Sus padres también se levantan a las siete.
8. ¿Qué hace su madre mientras su padre lee el periódico? Su madre prepara el desayuno mientras su padre lee el periódico.
9. ¿Qué hacen después de desayunar/del desayuno? Después de desayunar/del desayuno salen de la casa.
10. ¿Adónde (se) va su madre? Su madre se va de compras.
11. ¿Qué hacen por la tarde/noche? Por la noche se reunen todos de nuevo.
12. ¿Qué hacen después de cenar y mirar la tele? Después de cenar y mirar la tele se acuestan.

PRACTICE E: Free answer.

3. REFLEXIVE VERBS IN CONTEXT.

PRACTICE A:

VERB IN CONTEXT	INFINITIVE	SPANISH
1. goes to bed	to go to bed	acostarse (dipthong-"o" to "ue")
2. falls asleep	to fall asleep	dormirse (dipthong-"o" to "ue")
3. has	to have	tener (dipthong-"e" to "ie")
4. wakes up	to wake up	despertarse (dipthong-"e" to "ie")

5. gets up	to get up	levantarse
6. goes off	to go off	irse
7. brushes her teeth	To brush one´s teeth	cepillarse los dientes
8. looks at herself	To look at oneself	mirarse
9. bathes	To bathe/have a bath	bañarse
10. showers	To shower/have a shower	ducharse
11. is	To be	ser
12. feels	To feel	sentirse (dipthong-"e" to "ie")
13. brushes her hair	To brush one´s hair	cepillarse el pelo
14. dries her hair	To dry one´s hair	secarse el pelo
15. gets dressed	To get dressed	vestirse
16. puts on her make-up	To put on one´s make-up	pintarse
17. goes off	To go off	irse
18. makes herself	To make oneself	hacerse
19. sits down	To sit down	sentarse (dipthong-"e" to "ie")
20. reads	To read	leer
21. goes off	To go off	irse

PRACTICE B:

Todas las noches/cada noche María se acuesta a las once y media. Se duerme pronto y nunca tiene pesadillas. Se despierta a las siete pero nunca se levanta hasta las siete y cuarto. Se va al cuarto de baño donde se cepilla los dientes y se mira en el espejo. A veces, se baña, pero normalmente se ducha porque es más rápido y se sienta más limpia.

Después, se cepilla el pelo y se seca el pelo. María se viste y se pinta, después se va a la cocina donde se hace un café, se sienta y lee el periódico por diez minutos. Entonces se va a trabajar/ al trabajo.

PRACTICE C:

1. ¿A qué hora se acuesta María todas las noches/cada noche? María se acuesta a las once y media todas las noches/cada noche.
2. ¿Tiene pesadillas? Nunca tiene pesadillas.
3. ¿A qué hora se despierta todas las mañanas/cada mañana? Se despierta a las siete.
4. ¿Se levanta a esa hora? Nunca se levanta hasta las siete y cuarto.
5. ¿Qué hace en el cuarto de baño? Se cepilla los dientes y se mira en el espejo.
6. ¿Por qué se ducha normalmente? Normalmente se ducha porque es más rápido y se sienta más limpia.
7. ¿Qué hace después? Después, se cepilla el pelo y se seca el pelo.
8. ¿Qué hace en la cocina? Se hace un café, se sienta y lee el periódico por diez minutos.
9. ¿Qué hace después? Se va a trabajar/ al trabajo
10. ¿A qué hora te levantas (tú) normalmente? Free answer.

4. REFLEXIVE VERBS- CONVERSATION PRACTICE.

PRACTICE A:

1. to wash.
2. to feel.
3. to get/become nervous.
4. to go to bed.
5. to take off.
6. to get ill.
7. to put on.
8. to worry.
9. to get married.
10. to get angry.
11. to shower.
12. to bathe.
13. to brush.
14. to be called.
15. to get up.

PRACTICE B: Use them to translate the questions below. Practice asking and answering them with a friend. Remember to change the verb in the answer.

1. ¿Cómo te llamas?
2. ¿A qué hora te levantas normalmente?
3. ¿A qué hora te acuestas normalmente?

4. ¿Prefieres ducharte o bañarte?
5. ¿Cuándo te enfadas?
6. ¿Por qué te preocupas?
7. ¿Cómo te sientes hoy?
8. ¿Cuándo te pones nervioso?
9. ¿Te quitas los zapatos en la casa?
10. ¿Te enfermas a menudo?
11. ¿Cuántas veces al día te cepillas los dientes?
12. ¿Dónde se casa la gente en España?
13. ¿Te lavas el pelo todos los días?
14. ¿Qué ropa te pones en invierno?

FREE ANSWERS.

5. THE PRESENT PERFECT.

PRACTICE A:

1. ¿Cuánto tiempo has trabajado aqui?
2. Hoy he lavado el coche y limpiado la casa y mi marido ha mirado/visto la tele.
3. Este año hemos leido muchos libros distinctos.
4. Esta semana ha pagado doscientos euros por libros para la escuela.
5. ¿Habéis comido ya?
6. ¿Dónde están? Han ido a las tiendas.
7. Ha bedido demasiada cerveza y comido demasiado chocolate.
8. He comprado mis ropas aqui durante 13 años.
9. Has fregado/lavado los platos todavía?
10. Hemos estudiado mucho español este mes.

PRACTICE B:

1. Escribir - to write – escrito - written
2. Hacer - to do/make - hecho - made/done
3. Romper – to break - roto - broken
4. Ver -   to see/watch - visto – seen/watched
5. Volver - to return - vuelto - returned
6. Decir -   to say/tell - dicho – said/told
7. Abrir -   to open - abierto - opened
8. Morir - to die - muerto – died

9. Poner - to put - puesto – put
10. Cubrir – to cover - cubierto - covered
11. Freir – to fry - frito - fried

PRACTICE C:

1. ¿Cuántas cartas has escrito?
2. ¿Has visto a Juan?
3. ¿Quién ha roto la ventana?
4. ¿Qué has hecho?
5. ¿Qué te ha dicho Pedro?
6. He frito dos huevos esta mañana.
7. El Rey ha muerto.
8. Alguien ha abierto las ventanas.
9. No han vuelto todavía.
10. ¿Dónde habéis puesto las llaves?
11. La nieve ha cubierto las montañas.

PRACTICE D:

1. ¿Has visto una película? Si, he visto una película. No, no he visto una película.
2. ¿Has escrito una carta? Si, he escrito una carta. No, no he escrito una carta.
3. ¿Has leido un libro? Si, he leido un libro. No, no he leido un libro.
4. ¿Has dicho una mentira? Si, he dicho una mentira. No, no he dicho una mentira.
5. ¿Has frito una hamburguesa? Si, he frito una hamburguesa. No, no he frito una hamburguesa.
6. ¿Has comido pasta? Si, he comido pasta. No, no he comido pasta.
7. ¿Has bebido vino? Si, he bebido vino. No, no he bebido vino.
8. ¿Has roto algo? Si he roto algo. No, no he roto nada.
9. ¿Has hablado español con alguien? Si, he hablado español con alguien. No, no he hablado español con nadie.
10. ¿Has hecho los deberes? Si, he hecho mis deberes. No, no he hecho mis deberes.

6. THE PRESENT PERFECT IN CONTEXT

PRACTICE B:

VERB	INFINITIVE	ENGLISH	TENSE	PERSON
1. He llegado	llegar	To arrive	P. perfect	1st p.sing
2. hace	hacer	To do/ make	present	3rd p.sing
3. tengo	tener	To have	present	1st p.sing
4. contarte	contar	To tell	infinitive	infinitive
5. sabes	saber	To know	present	2nd p.sing
6. vivo	vivir	To live	present	1st p.sing
7. es	ser	To be	present	3rd p.sing
8. he tenido	tener	To have	P. perfect	1st p.sing
9. se llama	llamarse	To be called	present	3rd p.sing
10. es	ser	To be	present	3rd p.sing
11. hemos ido	ir	To go	P. perfect	1st p.plural
12. es	ser	To be	present	3rd p.sing
13. hemos visitado	visitar	To visit	P. perfect	1st p.plural
14. hemos estado	estar	To be	P. perfect	1st p.plural
15. tomando	tomar	To take	gerund	gerund
16. he pasado	pasar	To spend	P. perfect	1st p.sing
17. hablando	hablar	To speak	gerund	gerund
18. ha sido	ser	To be	P. perfect	3rd p.sing
19. tengo	tener	To have	present	1st p.sing
20. escuchar	escuchar	To listen	infinitive	infinitive
21. me acuesto	acostarse	**To go to bed**	present	1st p.sing
22. estoy	estar	To be	present	1st p.sing

PRACTICE C:

Hello Ana

I have arrived in Manchester only two days ago and I already have a thousand things to tell you. As you know, I live with a very nice English family especially the son David who besides is very good-looking.

This morning I have had my first English class. My teacher is called Carol and is blonde, tall and very nice. In the afternoon we have been to the Manchester Museum with the History teacher Alan, who is short, bald and a little serious and we have visited all the Egyptian rooms.

Then/later, we have been in the centre having some tapas in a Spanish restaurant. I have spent all day speaking in English, it has been great, although I still have some problems in listening to people. Now I am going to bed because I am very tired.

A hug, look after yourself,

Maite

PRACTICE D:

1. ¿Cuándo ha llegado Maite en Manchester? Ha llegado en Manchester hace solo dos días.
2. ¿Con quién vive? Vive con una familia inglesa.
3. ¿Qué ha tenido esta mañana? Esta mañana ha tenido su primera clase de inglés.
4. ¿Cómo se llama su profesor/a? Su profesora se llama Carol.
5. ¿Cómo es? Es rubia, alta y muy maja.
6. ¿A dónde han ido por la tarde? Por la tarde han ido al Museo de Manchester.
7. ¿Cómo es el profesor de historia? Es bajo, calvo y un poco serio.
8. ¿Qué han visitado? Han visitado todas las salas de Egipto.
9. ¿Dónde han estado después? Después han estado en el Centro tomando tapas.
10. ¿Cómo ha pasado todo el día? Ha pasado todo el día hablando en inglés.
11. ¿Qué problemas todavía tiene? Todavía tiene problemas en escuchar a la gente.
12. ¿Por qué se acuesta ahora? Se acuesta ahora porque está muy cansada.

7. DIRECT OBJECT PRONOUNS.

PRACTICE A:

1. Lo ha dado a María.
2. No lo ha dado a María.
3. (Os) quieren ver(os)
4. No las han visto está semana.
5. Lo ha buscado todo el día.

6. La limpio cada semana.
7. ¿Lo has entendido?
8. Nos ha visto.
9. John lo llama.
10. Lo dicen todo el tiempo
11. La ha llevado al aeropuerto.
12. Lo he llevado a casa.
13. No la puede vender.
14. ¿La has visto?
15. Los hemos olvidado.
16. Nos han olvidado.
17. Lo ha comprador esta semana.
18. La han pintado.
19. No lo ha hecho.
20. ¿Lo has hecho?
21. No las han escrito.
22. Lo entiendo.
23. La besa.
24. Nos invitan
25. Los veo.

PRACTICE B: TRANSLATE INTO SPANISH.

26. Paco la ama/ quiere.
27. Te necesito.
28. Las busca.
29. Nos visitan.
30. ¿Quién la conoce?
31. Nos han esperado mucho tiempo.
32. Me crees.
33. Os espero.
34. Nos dice.
35. Los chicos me han visto.
36. Lo veo.
37. Te eligen.
38. No lo oigo.
39. No la quieren.
40. No la podemos ver.
41. No los visito a menudo.
42. No lo quiere hacer.

43. La he puesto en la mesa.
44. No los quiero aqui.
45. Tenéis que hacerlo cada día.
46. Lo sabes.
47. Lo encuentra difícil.
48. Los odiamos.
49. Las he visto hoy.
50. Los llevas al aeropuerto cada vez.

8. DIRECT OBJECT PRONOUNS IN CONTEXT.

PRACTICE A:

VERB	INFINITIVE	SPANISH	TENSE	PERSON
1. I want	To want	querer	present	1st p. sing.
2. to visit	To visit	visitar	infinitive	infinitive
3. I haven´t seen	To see	ver	p.perfect	1st p. sing.
4. I need	To need	necesitar	present	1st p. sing.
5. to call	To call	llamar	infinitive	infinitive
6. I think	To think	pensar	present	1st p. sing.
7. has left	To leave	dejar	p.perfect	3rd p.sing.
8. I have called	To call	llamar	p.perfect	1st p. sing.
9. I have been	To go	ir	p.perfect	1st p. sing.
10. I don´t know	To know	saber	present	1st p. sing.
11. is	To be	estar	present	3rd p.sing.
12. I have looked for	To look for	buscar	p.perfect	1st p. sing.
13. I haven´t been able	To be able	poder	p.perfect	1st p. sing.
14. to find	To find	encontrar	infinitive	infinitive
15. says	To say	decir	present	3rd p.sing.
16. he has gone	To go	ir	p.perfect	3rd p.sing.
17. he hasn´t said	To say	decir	p.perfect	3rd p.sing.
18. says	To say	decir	present	3rd p.sing.
19. he has wanted	To want	querer	p.perfect	3rd p.sing.

20. to go	To go	ir	infinitive	infinitive
21. he thinks	To think	pensar	present	3rd p.sing.
22. he is	To be	estar	present	3rd p.sing.
23. I want	To want	querer	present	1st p. sing.
24. to talk	To talk	hablar	infinitive	infinitive
25. she has given	To give	dar	p.perfect	3rd p.sing.
26. I need	To need	necesitar	present	1st p. sing.
27. I have to	To have to	tener que	present	1st p. sing.
28. see	To see	ver	infinitive	infinitive
29. take	To take	llevar	infinitive	infinitive
30. lunch	To have lunch	comer	infinitive	infinitive
31. chat	To chat	charlar	infinitive	infinitive
32. I haven't argued	To argue	discutir	p.perfect	1st p. sing.
33. I don't understand	To understand	comprender /entender	present	1st p. sing.
34. has left	To leave	dejar	p.perfect	3rd p.sing.
35. saying	To say	decir	infinitive	infinitive
36. I have left	To leave	dejar	p.perfect	1st p. sing.
37. I need	To need	necesitar	present	1st p. sing.
38. I have also left	To leave	dejar	p. present	1st p. sing.
39. I need	To need	necesitar	present	1st p. sing.
40. I can't	To can	poder	present	1st p.sing.
41. get	To get	obtener	infinitive	infinitive
42. can	To can	poder	present	3rd p.sing.
43. get	To get	obtener	infinitive	infinitive
44. he can	To can	poder	present	3rd p.sing.
45. get	To get	obtener	infinitive	infinitive

PRACTICE B:

Quiero visitar a mi hermana por que no la he visto por más que dos semanas. Necesito llamarla porque pienso que mi novio me ha dejado. Lo he llamado por teléfono, he ido a su casa, pero no sé donde está. Lo he buscado en su bar local, en su oficina, y en la casa de sus padres pero no (lo) he podido encontrar(lo).

Su hermano dice que se ha ido de vacaciones, pero no me ha dicho nada. Dice que ha querido ir a España durante mucho tiempo y piensa que está allí ahora. Quiero hablar con mi hermana porque siempre me ha dado consejos buenos y los necesito ahora. Tengo que verla y llevarla a comer para charlar.

No he discutido con él entonces no comprendo por que me ha dejado sin decir nada. He dejado mis gafas de sol en su casa y las necesito para mis vacaciones la semana que viene. También he dejado mi bolso negro allí y lo necesito para una fiesta el sábado por la noche. Si no puedo obtenerlo el hermano de mi novio puede obtenerlo para mí. También mis gafas de sol, puede obtenerlas para mí también.

PRACTICE C:

1. ¿Por qué quiere visitar a su hermana? Quiere visitar a su hermana porque no la ha visto por más que dos semanas.
2. ¿Por qué necesita llamarla? Necesita llamarla porque piensa que su novio la ha dejado.
3. ¿Dónde ha buscado a su novio? Lo ha buscado en su bar local, en su oficina, y en la casa de sus padres.
4. ¿Qué dice el hermano de su novio? El hermano de su novio dice que se ha ido de vacaciones.
5. ¿Por qué quiere hablar con su hermana? Quiere hablar con su hermana porque siempre ha dado consejos buenos y los necesita ahora.
6. ¿Dónde la necesita llevar y por qué? Necesita llevarla a comer para charlar.
7. ¿Ha discutido con él? No ha discutido con él.
8. ¿Qué ha dejado en su casa? Ha dejado sus gafas de sol en su casa.
9. ¿Por qué las necesita? Las necesita para sus vacaciones la semana que viene.
10. ¿Qué ha dejado allí también? También ha dejado su bolso negro alli.
11. ¿Por qué lo necesita? Lo necesita para una fiesta el sábado por la noche.
12. ¿Quién puede obtenerlos para ella? El hermano de su novio puede obtenerlos para ella.

10. THE BROKEN FLOWER VASE

PRACTICE A:

Es una tarde bonita de primavera y Señor Martínez ha vuelto de la oficina. Esta tarde tiene que preparar la cena porque su esposa/ mujer (se) ha ido a Barcelona para pasar unas días con sus padres. Pedro y María han vuelto

antes de su padre. María ya ha empezado/ comenzado a preparar la cena y Pedro ha puesto la mesa. Señor Martínez ha abierto la puerta del salón y ha entrado, pero no se ha sentado porque no puede encontrar su periódico.

Señor Martinez- Pedro, ¿has visto mi periódico? He olvidado donde lo he puesto.
Pedro - No lo he visto Papá. Quizás lo has dejado en la cocina.
Maria - ¿Qué buscáis?
Señor. Martínez - Mi periódico- Quiero leer un poco antes de cenar
María - - Lo has dejado en la mesita/ mesa pequeña. ¿Lo ves? A la izquierda de ese florero azul por allí...
Señor. Martínez - "Ah, sí, lo veo. Gracias María.

Va a cogerlo, pero resbala y golpea conta la mesa. El floreo se cae al suelo.

María - Papá!! ¿Qué has hecho? ¿Está roto el florero?
Sñr. Martínez - Sí, lo he roto.
Maria - Oh, Papá!! Mamá siempre ha dicho que es su florero favorito. Es un regalo de su tia Lourdes.
Señor. Martínez - A ver/ vamos a ver. Vuestra madre vuelve el viernes. Tenemos cuatro días para encontrar otro.

El día siguiente Señor Martínez explica a su amigo Jordi que ha hecho. Él (lo) quiere ayudar(lo) y dice que hay una tienda en el centro de la ciudad dende venden este tipo de cerámica.

-No he tenido ningún suerte- dice a Jordi el día siguiente cuando vuelve/ regresa de la oficina. – Han vendido todos-.

Sus hijos/ niños no han tenido suerte tampoco. Han visitado muchas tiendas sin encontrar nada.
-Juan nos ha ayudado- dice Pedro- pero no hemos encontrado nada-

Señora Martínez Vuelve/ regresa de Barcelona el viernes y los otros van a la estación para recibirla. Con ella tiene su maleta y un paquete grande
Mrs. Martinez returns from Barcelona on Friday and the others go to the station to greet her. With her she has her suitcase and a large parcel. No quiere abrirlo antes de llegar a casa. En camino a casa su marido/ esposo explica como ha roto el florero. (Ella) no dice nada. En la casa pone el paquete encima de/ en/ sobre la mesa, saca las tijeras, y corta la cuerda alrededor del paquete. Lo abre y saca otro florero.
-Lo he comprado en Barcelona- dice (ella)- Entonces/ Así que te perdono.

PRACTICE B:

1. ¿Cómo es la tarde? Es bonita.
2. ¿De dónde ha vuelto Señor Martínez? Ha vuelto de la oficina.
3. ¿Por qué tiene que preparar la cena esta tarde? Porque su esposa/ mujer (se) ha ido a Barcelona para pasar unos días con sus padres.
4. ¿Quién ha vuelto antes de él? Pedro y María han vuelto antes de él.
5. ¿Quién ya ha empezado preparar la cena? María.
6. ¿Qué ha hecho Pedro? Ha puesto la mesa.
7. ¿Por qué no se ha sentado Señor Martínez? No encuentra su periódico.
8. ¿Lo ha visto Pedro? No, no lo ha visto.
9. ¿Dónde lo ha dejado? En la mesa pequeña.
10. ¿Qué pasa cuando va a conseguirlo? Resbala y tropieza contra la mesa.
11. ¿Está roto el florero? Si.
12. ¿Cuándo vuelve Señora Martínez? El viernes.
13. ¿A quién explica el Señor Martínez que ha hecho? A su amigo Jordi.
14. ¿Dónde hay una tienda que vende este tipo de cerámica? En el centro de la ciudad.
15. ¿Ha tenido suerte? No.
16. ¿Han tenido suerte los niños? No.
17. ¿Quién los ha ayudado? Juan.
18. ¿A quién reciben a la estación? A Señora Martínez.
19. ¿Qué tiene con ella? Un paquete.
20. ¿Qué explica su marido en camino a la estación? Como ha roto el florero.
21. ¿Qué dice? No dice nada.
22. ¿Qué hace en la casa? Pone el paquete en la mesa.
23. ¿Qué saca? Otro florero.
24. Dónde lo ha comprado? Lo ha comprado en Barcelona.

10. CONVERSATION PRACTICE PRESENT PERFECT- "EVER"/"ALGUNA VEZ".

PRACTICE A: (FREE ANSWERS)

1. ¿Has estado en Méjico alguna vez?
2. ¿Has visto un OVNI alguna vez?
3. ¿Has visto un fantasma alguna vez?
4. ¿Has vivido en otro país alguna vez?
5. ¿Has visto un robo alguna vez?
6. ¿Has ganado un premio alguna vez?
7. ¿Has perdido un vuelo o tren alguna vez?
8. ¿Has perdido todo tu dinero alguna vez?
9. ¿Has tenido un acidente alguna vez?
10. ¿Has estudiado alemán alguna vez?
11. ¿Has tenido un perro alguna vez?
12. ¿Has conocido a alguien famoso alguna vez?
13. ¿Has ido a los Estados Unidos alguna vez?
14. ¿Has hecho algo tonto alguna vez?
15. ¿Has escrito un poema alguna vez?
16. ¿Has cocinado para más que 20 personas alguna vez?
17. ¿Has comprado algo muy caro alguna vez?
18. ¿Has comprado un coche rojo alguna vez?
19. ¿Has hablado con un desconocido en un tren alguna vez?
20. ¿Has dicho una mentira alguna vez?

11. SER AND ESTAR- THE 2 VERBS "TO BE"- PRESENT TENSE AND PRESENT PERFECT.

PRACTICE A:

1. Somos ingleses.
2. La mesa es cuadrada.
3. Han sido profesores durante más que veinte años.
4. Siempre ha sido alta.
5. Son de España.
6. ¿Quién es Juan?
7. Nunca he sido su amigo.
8. ¿Son españoles?
9. ¿Habéis sido estudiantes alguna vez?
10. ¿Cuándo es la clase?

PRACTICE B:
1. Hemos estado en Inglaterra.
2. La mesa está sucia.
3. ¿Estás cansado?
4. ¿Estáis felices/contentos?
5. Ella está en el jardín.
6. Han estado enfermos.
7. He estado muy triste.
8. Paris está en Francia.
9. Los niños están enfermos.
10. Esta manzana está negra.

PRACTICE C:
1. ¿De dónde eres?
2. ¿Dónde han estado?
3. ¿Dónde está mi coche?
4. La pelota es roja.
5. Jordi y María han estado muy cansados hoy.
6. ¿Cómo estás?
7. ¿Cómo es Pedro?
8. ¿Con quién estamos?
9. Los gatos han estado en la terraza/el patio toda la mañana.
10. La casa está sucia.
11. José siempre ha sido un hombre muy guapo.
12. María y Belén son rubias.
13. Manuel y Begoña han sido abogados en la ciudad desde hace dos mil cinco.
14. Ha sido mi mejor amigo durante diez años.
15. ¿Cuando es la clase de Español?

12. THE PRETERITE/SIMPLE PAST TENSE-REGULAR VERBS.

PRACTICE A:
NO ACCENTS

1. mirar	To watch, look at	2. hablar	To speak	3. ver	To see/watch
mir	é	habl	é	v	i
mir	aste	habl	aste	v	iste

mir	ó	habl	ó	v	io
mir	amos	habl	amos	v	imos
mir	asteis	habl	asteis	v	isteis
mir	aron	habl	aron	v	ieron

4. enviar	To send	5. vivir	To live	6. comer	To eat
envi	é	viv	í	com	í
envi	aste	viv	iste	com	iste
envi	ó	viv	ió	com	ió
envi	amos	viv	imos	com	imos
envi	asteis	viv	isteis	com	isteis
envi	aron	viv	ieron	com	ieron

7. beber	To drink	8. limpiar	To clean	9. recibir	To receive
beb	í	limpi	é	recib	í
beb	iste	limpi	aste	recib	iste
beb	ió	limpi	ó	recib	ió
beb	imos	limpi	amos	recib	imos
beb	isteis	limpi	asteis	recib	isteis
beb	ieron	limpi	aron	recib	ieron

10. escuchar	To listen
escuch	é
escuch	aste
escuch	ó
escuch	amos
escuch	asteis

escuch	aron

PRACTICE B:

1. Anoche hablé con Juan.
2. Vi al médico ayer.
3. Escuchamos mucho español el mes pasado.
4. Anteayer recibí una carta.
5. Miramos muchas casas en Francia en verano.
6. Comiste en un restaurante.
7. Limpié la casa ayer.
8. Viví en Inglaterra en mil novecientos ochenta y ocho.
9. Bebisteis cerveza en la fiesta anoche.
10. Mandamos/enviamos muchos correos electrónicos ayer.
11. ¿Visteis la tormenta anteayer?
12. Limpiaron el coche la semana pasada.
13. Bailó en la disco el viernes por la noche.
14. Bebió demasiado vino el fin de semana.
15. ¿Compraste algo el sábado?
16. ¿Con quién hablaste en la fiesta?

13. PRETERITE TENSE - IRREGULAR VERBS.

PRACTICE A:

1. hacer – do/make

| hice |
| hiciste |
| hizo |
| hicimos |
| hicisteis |
| hicieron |

2. poner - put

| puse |
| pusiste |
| puso |
| pusimos |
| pusisteis |
| pusieron |

3. poder- be able

| pude |
| pudiste |
| pudo |
| pudimos |
| pudisteis |
| pudieron |

4. saber- know

| supe |
| supiste |
| supo |
| supimos |
| supisteis |
| supieron |

5. estar- be

| estuve |
| estuviste |
| estuvo |
| estuvimos |
| estuvisteis |
| estuvieron |

6. dar- give

| di |
| diste |
| dio |
| dimos |
| disteis |
| dieron |

7. tener- have	8. decir- say/tell	9. conducir- drive
tuve	dije	conduje
tuviste	dijiste	condujiste
tuvo	dijo	condujo
tuvimos	dijimos	condujimos
tuvisteis	dijisteis	condujisteis
tuvieron	dijeron	condujeron

10. traer- bring	11. querer - want	12. venir- come
traje	quise	vine
trajiste	quisiste	viniste
trajo	quiso	vino
trajimos	quisimos	vinimos
trajisteis	quisisteis	vinisteis
trajeron	quisieron	vinieron

PRACTICE B:

1. ¿Qué hiciste anoche?
2. ¿Dónde pusiste el periódico?
3. Dio un regalo a Carmen.
4. Condujimos aquí ayer.
5. Vinieron a España en agosto.
6. Quiso comprar la casa el año pasado.
7. En mil novecientos noventa y nueve tuve mi primer hijo.
8. El camarero trajo la carta a la mesa.
9. No pudimos dormir anoche.
10. ¿Qué dijisteis a Pablo?
11. ¿Supiste abrir la puerta?
12. ¿Dónde estuviste el viernes a las cuatro?
13. ¿Por qué diste la llave a Juan?
14. Conduje al mercadillo.
15. Nos trajeron una botella de vino.
16. No pudisteis hacerlo/No lo pudisteis hacer.
17. Puso el papel en la papelera.
18. Lo reconozco/admito. Lo hice.
19. Se hizo una taza de café ayer por la tarde.
20. Se pusieron los sombreros y guantes para ir al parque.

14. SER AND IR - PRETERITE/ PAST SIMPLE TENSE.

PRACTICE A:

1. Fui estudiante en mil novecientos setenta y nueve.
2. Me fui a las tiendas ayer.
3. ¿Fuiste a la fiesta anoche?
4. La casa fue barata hace 5 años.
5. El sábado pasado fueron a la casa de Juan.
6. La clase fue muy interesante.
7. ¿Fuisteis al mercadillo el sábado?
8. Fuimos a casa a las ocho.
9. ¿Quién fue el mejor estudiante ayer?
10. Pedro y María fueron esposos/marido y mujer durante cinco años, pero nunca fueron a Inglaterra.

15. CONVERSATION PRACTICE PRETERITE/ SIMPLE PAST.

PRACTICE A:

1. ¿Qué hiciste anoche?
2. ¿A qué hora te levantaste el domingo pasado?
3. ¿Adónde fuiste anteayer?
4. ¿Con quién hablaste el sábado?
5. ¿Qué te dio la familia para tu último cumpleaños?
6. ¿Qué película viste el mes pasado?
7. ¿Qué te pusiste ayer?
8. ¿Cuándo tuviste tu primera clase de español?
9. ¿A qué hora cenaste anoche?
10. ¿Por qué viniste a España?
11. ¿A qué hora te acostaste el lunes pasado?
12. ¿Te duchaste ayer?
13. ¿A quién viste el fin de semana?
14. ¿Dónde hablaste español ayer?
15. ¿Qué fue el último libro que leíste?

FREE ANSWERS.

16. PRETERITE IN CONTEXT.

PRACTICE B:

VERB	INFINITIVE	ENGLISH	TENSE	PERSON
1. me levanté	levantarse	To get up	preterite	1st p. sing.
2. desayuné	desayunar	To breakfast	preterite	1st p. sing.
3. trabajé	trabajar	To work	preterite	1st p. sing.
4. vuelvo	volver	To return	present	1st p. sing.
5. comer	comer	To have lunch	infinitive	infinitive
6. comí	comer	To have lunch	preterite	1st p. sing.
7. fuimos	ir	To go	preterite	1st p. plur.
8. comprar	comprar	To buy	infinitive	infinitive
9. llegué	llegar	To arrive	preterite	1st p. sing.
10. entré	entrar	To enter	preterite	1st p. sing.
11. ví	ver	To see	preterite	1st p. sing.
12. cantaron	cantar	To sing	preterite	3rd p. plur.
13. regalaron	regalar	To give (as a gift)	preterite	3rd p. plur.
14. estuve	estar	To be	preterite	1st p. sing.
15. visitamos	visitar	To visit	preterite	1st p. plur.
16. cenamos	cenar	To dine	preterite	1st p. plur.
17. vinieron	venir	To come	preterite	3rd p. plur.
18. cenar	cenar	To dine	infinitive	infinitive
19. pasé	pasar	To spend	preterite	1st p.sing

PRACTICE C:

Yesterday, the day of my birthday, I got up at 7, like every day. I had breakfast with my husband at home/in the house and worked all morning as always. Normally at midday I return home for lunch but yesterday I had lunch in a restaurant, Meso de Miguel, with my husband Paco. Then/later we went to El Corte Inglés to buy a present for me and I arrived at the office a little late.

When I entered my office I saw a big birthday cake on the table with two bottles of champagne. All my workmates sang "happy birthday" and presented me with a bracelet from all of them. I was very happy.

In the evening we visited my parents and we had dinner with them. My brothers and sisters and cousins also came to have dinner with us. I had a very nice day.

PRACTICE D: Translate these questions into Spanish and answer in Spanish.

1. ¿Qué día fue ayer? Ayer fue el cumpleaños de Carmen.
2. ¿A qué hora se levantó Carmen? Se levantó a las siete.
3. ¿Con quién desayunó y dónde? Desayunó con su marido en la casa.
4. ¿Dónde come normalmente? Normalmente a mediodía vuelve a casa para comer/come en la casa.
5. ¿Dónde comió ayer y con quién? Comió en un restaurante, Mesón de Miguel, con su marido Paco.
6. ¿Adónde fueron entonces y por qué? Luego fueron al Corte Inglés para comprar un regalo para ella.
7. ¿Qué vio cuando entró en la oficina? Vio un pastel de cumpleaños grande en la mesa con dos botellas de champán.
8. ¿Qué cantaron los compañeros? Todos sus/los compañeros cantaron "Cumpleaños Feliz".
9. ¿Qué le regalaron? Le regalaron una pulsera en nombre de todos ellos.
10. ¿Qué hicieron por la tarde? Por la tarde visitaron a sus padres y cenaron con ellos.
11. ¿Quién/es vino/ieron para cenar también? También vinieron sus hermanos y primos para cenar con ellos.
12. ¿Pasó bien el día? Si, Pasó un día muy agradable.

PRACTICE E: FREE ANSWER.

17. UNA TARDE INOLVIDABLE

PRACTICE A:

VERB	INFINITIVE	ENGLISH	TENSE	PERSON
1. trabajo	trabajar	To work	present	1st p. sing
2. soy	ser	To be	present	1st p. sing
3. paso	pasar		present	1st p. sing
4. he trabajado	trabajar	To work	p. perfect	1st p. sing
5. hace	hacer	To do/make(ago)	present	3rd p.sing
6. empecé	empezar	To start	preterite	1st p. sing

7. sentir	sentir	To feel		infinitive
8. Fui	ir	To go	preterite	1st p. sing
9. recomendó	recomendar	To recommend	preterite	3rd p.sing
10. hacer	hacer	To do		infinitive
11. Probé	probar	To try	preterite	1st p. sing
12. encontré	encontrar	To find	preterite	1st p. sing
13. Me apunté	apuntarse	To enrol	preterite	1st p. sing
14. me aburrí	aburrirse	To get bored	preterite	1st p. sing
15. empeoraron	empeorar	To get worse	preterite	3rd p. plural
16. invitó	invitar	To invite	preterite	3rd p.sing
17. ver	ver	To see		infinitive
18. Fue	ser	To be	preterite	3rd p.sing
19. gritaron	gritar	To shout	preterite	3rd p. plural
20. parar	parar	To stop		infinitive
21. animar	animar	To encourage		infinitive
22. Insultaron	insultar	To insult	preterite	3rd p. plural
23. saltaron	saltar	To jump	preterite	3rd p. plural
24. metimos	meter	To put in	preterite	1st p. plural
25. Ganamos	ganar	To win	preterite	1st p. plural
26. Tuvimos	tener	To have	preterite	1st p. plural
27. pasamos	pasar	To pass	preterite	1st p. plural
28. veo	ver	I see/ watch	present	1st p. sing
29. viajo	viajar	To travel	present	1st p. sing
30. animar	animar	To encourage		infinitive
31. Soy	ser	To be	present	1st p. sing
32. me levanto	levantarse	To get up	present	1st p. sing
33. se acabaron	acabarse	To finish	preterite	3rd p. plural

PRACTICE B:

I work in an Insurance Company, I am a Clerk/ admin assistant etc. I spend 5 days a week , during nearly 7 hours, sitting at a desk/ table. I have worked there for 14 years.

Two years ago, I started to feel depressed. I went to the doctor, and he recommended me to exercise. I tried tennis, but I found it very difficult. I enrolled in a gym, but I got bored quickly. My depression got worse.

One day, a workmate/ colleague invited me to watch a football game between the local team and an away team. It was an unforgettable afternoon. The spectators shouted non-stop to encourage/ cheer on our team. They insulted the referee for some fouls against our team and jumped for joy with the goal we out in/ scored. We won. We had a big party. We had a great time.

Since then, I see all my team's matches, home and away. Some weekends I travel up to 1,500 kilometres to cheer on our team. I am a typical fan. On Monday mornings I get up tired/ exhausted, but happy. And my depression has ended!!

PRACTICE C:

1. ¿Dónde trabaja y qué hace? Trabaja en una compañia de seguros, es oficinista.
2. ¿Cómo pasa la semana? Pasa la semana sentado a una mesa.
3. ¿Cuánto tiempo ha trabajado alli? Ha trabajo allí durante catorce años.
4. ¿Qué pasó hace dos años? Empezó a sentir depresiones.
5. ¿Qué recomendó el médico? Le recomendó hacer ejercicio.
6. ¿Cómo encontró el tennis? Lo encontró difícil.
7. ¿Le gustó el gimnasio? No, se aburrió pronto.
8. ¿Qué pasó un día? Un compañero de trabajo lo/le invitó a ver un partido de fútbol.
9. ¿Cómo fue la tarde? Fue una tarde inolvidable.
10. ¿Qué hicieron los espectadores? Gritaron sin parar para animar su equipo. Insultaron al árbitro por algunos faltas contra los suyos y saltaron de alegría con el gol que metieron.
11. ¿Ganaron? Sí, ganaron.
12. ¿Qué hace (él) algunos fines de semana? Viaja hasta 1,500 kilómetros para animar a su equipo.
13. ¿Cçomo se levanta los lunes por la mañana? Se levanta agotado pero felíz.
14. ¿Todavía tiene depresiones? No, se acabaron los depresiones

18. COMPARISON OF SER AND ESTAR-PRETERITE.

PRACTICE A:

1. La boda fue el sábado.
2. La comida estuvo en un restaurante en el centro de la ciudad. Fue buena.
3. En la boda, la cubertería que estuvo en la mesa fue de plata.
4. El examen estuvo en la escuela/el colegio y fue muy difícil.
5. En mil novecientos noventa y nueve fui muy joven y fui estudiante.

6. La última vez que estuve en Londres tuve una experiencia fatal/terrible.
7. Fui presidente del club durante un año.
8. ¿Quién fue el ganador ayer?
9. Fue una fiesta terrible.
10. Fue mi mejor amigo durante/por diez años.

19. ALGO/NADA.

PRACTICE A:

1. ¿Quieres algo de comer?
   Sí, quiero algo.
   No, no quiero nada.

2. ¿Saben algo de Pedro?
   Sí, saben algo.
   No, no saben nada.

3. ¿Te han dicho algo de la casa?
   Sí, me han dicho algo.
   No, no me han dicho nada.

4. ¿Comprendiste/entendiste algo en español?
   Sí, comprendí/ entendí algo.
   No, no comprendí/ entendí nada.

5. ¿Vas a comprar algo?
   Sí, voy a comprar algo.
   No, no voy a comprar nada.

6. ¿Has visto algo?
   Si, he visto algo.
   No, no he visto nada.

7. ¿Has hecho algo esta semana?
   Sí, he hecho algo.
   No, no he hecho nada.

8. ¿Compraste algo ayer?
   Si, compré algo.
   No, no compré nada.

9. ¿Cocinó algo para tí?
    Sí, cocinó algo para mí.
    No, no cocinó nada para mí.

10. ¿Hiciste algo para él?
    Sí, hice algo para él.
    No, no hice nada para él.

11. ¿Ha escrito algo?
    No, no ha escrito nada.
    Sí, ha escrito algo.

12. ¿Rompieron algo en la fiesta?
    No, no rompieron nada.
    Sí, rompieron algo.

13. ¿Ves algo?
    Sí, veo algo.
    No, no veo nada.

14. ¿Quieres algo?
    Sí, quiero algo.
    No, no quiero nada.

15. ¿Recordaste algo?
    Sí, recordé algo.
    No, no recordé nada.

20. ALGUIEN/NADIE.

PRACTICE A:

1. ¿Hay alguien en el restaurante?
    Sí, hay alguien.
    No, no hay nadie.

2. ¿Está con alguien?
    Sí, está con alguien.
    No, no está con nadie.

3. ¿Has visto a alguien?
   Sí, he visto a alguien.
   No, no he visto a nadie.

4. ¿Van a la fiesta con alguien?
   Sí, van a la fiesta con alguien.
   No, no van a la fiesta con nadie.

5. ¿Invitaste a alguien?
   Sí, invité a alguien.
   No, no invité a nadie.

6. ¿Habéis hablado con alguien?
   Sí, hemos hablado con alguien.
   No, no hemos hablado con nadie.

7. ¿Trabajó alguien allí?
   Sí, alguien trabajó allí.
   No, nadie trabajó allí.

8. ¿Hablaste con alguien en español?
   Sí, hablé con alguien.
   No, no hablé con nadie en español.

9. ¿Te gusta alguien?
   Sí, me gusta alguien.
   No, no me gusta nadie.

10. ¿Vino alguien a la fiesta?
    Sí, vino alguien.
    No, no vino nadie.

11. ¿Has besado a alguien?
    Sí, he besado a alguien.
    No, no he besado a nadie.

12. ¿Quieres a alguien?
    Sí, quiero a alguien.
    No, no quiero a nadie.

13. ¿Bailaste con alguien?

Sí, bailé con alguien.
No, no bailé con nadie.

14. ¿Ha matado a alguien?
    No, no ha matado a nadie.
    Sí, ha matado a alguien.

15. ¿Necesitas a alguien?
    Sí, necesito a alguien.
    No, no necesito a nadie.

16. ¿Lo ha hecho alguien para tí?
    Sí, alguien lo ha hecho para mí.
    No, nadie lo ha hecho para mí.

21. THE IMPERFECT TENSE.

PRACTICE A:

1. Hablabamos por teléfono cada/todas las noches.
2. El sol brillaba.
3. Cuando era niño/a, vivía en Inglaterra.
4. Escuchaban la radio.
5. ¿Dónde jugabas cuando eras niño/a?
6. (Yo) nadaba en el mar.
7. (Ella) tenía un perro.
8. Su profesor/a gritaba todo el tiempo.
9. ¿Dónde trabajabas?
10. Carmen limpiaba la casa los fines de semana.
11. Siempre se levantaban a las siete para ir a trabajar/al trabajo.
12. Me vestía.
13. Su padre era contable.
14. Miraba/veía mi programa favorito en la tele.
15. Hacía mucho sol en España.

22. THE IMPERFECT TENSE IN CONTEXT.

PRACTICE B:

VERB	INFINITIVE	ENGLISH	TENSE	PERSON
1. era	ser	To be	imperfect	1st p. sing.

2. vivía	vivir	To live	imperfect	1st p. sing.
3. tenía	tener	To have	imperfect	1st p. sing.
4. tenían	tener	To have	imperfect	3rd p. plural
5. iba	ir	To go	imperfect	1st p. sing.
6. gustaba	gustar	To please	imperfect	3rd p. sing.
7. jugaba	jugar	To play	imperfect	1st p. sing.
8. era	ser	To be	imperfect	3rd p. sing.
9. habían	haber	To have	imperfect	3rd p. plural
10. había	haber	To have	imperfect	3rd p. sing.
11. me acuerdo	acordarse	To remember	present	1st p. sing.
12. hizo	hacer	To do/make	preterite	3rd p. sing.
13. nevó	nevar	To snow	preterite	3rd p. sing.
14. pudimos	poder	To be able	preterite	1st p. plural.
15. jugar	jugar	To play	infinitive	infinitive
16. quería	querer	To want	imperfect	1st p. sing
17. dejaban	dejar	To let	imperfect	3rd p. plural.
18. era	ser	To be	imperfect	3rd p. sing.
19. trabajaba	trabajar	To work	imperfect	3rd p. sing.
20. ganaba	ganar	To earn	imperfect	3rd p. sing.
21. trabajaba	trabajar	To work	imperfect	3rd p. sing.
22. tenían	tener	To have	imperfect	3rd p. plural.
23. tenían	tener	To have	imperfect	3rd p. plural.
24. teníamos	tener	To have	imperfect	1st p. plural.
25. estábamos	estar	To be	imperfect	1st p. plural.

PRACTICE C:

When I was a child/girl, I lived in England with my family. I had four siblings, two brothers and two sisters. They were all older than me.

I used to go/went to the local school, and I liked it a lot. I used to play/played in the street and in the countryside. It was safer then for children and there weren´t so many cars. There was a big park near to my house and I remember very well one year when it was very cold and snowed a lot. We could play in the snow every day.

I always wanted a dog, but my parents wouldn´t let me. My father was strict, but nice. He worked/used to work in an office and he never earned much money. My mother worked in the house. They both had bicycles, they never had a car.

We never had much money, but we were more or less happy.

PRACTICE D:

1. ¿Dónde vivía cuando era niña? Vivía en Manchester.
2. ¿Cuántos hermanos tenía? Tenía cuatro hermanos.
3. ¿Tenían menos años que ella? No, todos tenían más años que ella.
4. ¿Adónde iba a la escuela? Iba a la escuela en su barrio.
5. ¿Dónde jugaba? Jugaba en las calles y en el campo.
6. ¿De qué se acuerda muy bien? Se acuerda muy bien de un año cuando hizo mucho frio y nevó mucho.
7. ¿Cuándo pudieron jugar en la nieve? Pudieron jugar en la nieve todos los días.
8. ¿Qué siempre quería? Siempre quería un perro.
9. ¿Cómo era su padre? Su padre era estricto, pero simpático.
10. ¿Dónde trabajaba? Trabajaba en una oficina.
11. ¿Dónde trabajaba su madre? Trabajaba en la casa.
12. ¿Estaban felices/contentos? Sí, más o menos estaban felices.

PRACTICE E: FREE ANSWER

23. IMPERFECT TENSE- CONVERSATION PRACTICE.

PRACTICE A:

1. ¿Dónde vivías en el Reino Unido?
2. ¿Adónde ibas a la escuela?
3. ¿Dónde jugabas?
4. ¿A qué hora te levantabas cuando trabajabas?
5. ¿Qué hacías los domingos?
6. ¿Dónde comprabas la ropa?
7. ¿Qué te ponías en el invierno?
8. ¿Qué veías/mirabas en la tele los sábados por la noche?
9. ¿Comías en los restaurantes a menudo?

10. ¿Jugabas deportes?
11. ¿Cuándo ibas de vacaciones?
12. ¿Por qué querías venir a España?
13. ¿Podías hablar el español antes de venir aquí?
14. Cuando eras niño/a, ¿sabías nadar?
15. ¿Dónde estaba tu primera casa?
16. ¿De qué color era tu primer coche?
17. ¿Siempre hacías los deberes?
18. ¿Te portabas bien en la escuela?
19. Cuando eras niño/a, ¿tenías animales?
20. ¿Qué querías ser?

24. COMPARISON OF SER AND ESTAR-IMPERFECT TENSE.

PRACTICE A:

1. ¿Cómo era el padre de Carlos?
2. ¿Dónde estabas? Te buscaba.
3. Era actríz que me gustaba mucho.
4. Mi casa antigua estaba en el centro de la ciudad.
5. Siempre estaban de buen humor y nos decían/contaban historias graciosas/cuentos graciosos/chistes.
6. (Yo) Estaba enferma y no podía ir a la fiesta.
7. Quería comprar los zapatos pero eran muy caros.
8. ¿Por qué estaba en ese coche?
9. Juan era muy alto y guapo.
10. Cuando estaba en España, era policía.

PRACTICE B:

1. (a) Cada/todos los lunes estaba enferma y no podía trabajar.
   (b) Cada/todos los lunes las colas eran largas.

2. (a) Los viernes estaba en el trabajo hasta las ocho.
   (b) Los viernes las bebidas eran baratas.

3. (a) Cada/todas las semanas (yo) estaba allí en su casa.
   (b) Cada/todas las semanas eran más caras.

4. (a) Cuando (yo) era niño/a siempre jugaba en el parque.
   (b) Cuando (yo) era niño/a siempre estaba en el parque.

5. (a) Siempre era alta para su edad.
   (b) Las tiendas siempre estaban cerradas los domingos.

6. (a) Nunca eran bailadores muy buenos.
   (b) Nunca estabáis aqui cuando os necesitaba.

7. (a) (Yo) Nunca era estricto/a.
   (b) Nunca estaban en clase.

8. (a) (Yo) era cantante en un bar.
   (b) (Él) siempre estaba felíz/contento cuando ella estaba allí.

9. (a) Siempre erais muy listos/inteligentes.
   (b) Estabáis a menudo en la playa cuando yo estaba allí.

10. (a) Cada año las vacaciones eran más y más caras.
    (b) Cada año estaban abiertos más tarde.

25. VERB PRACTICE.

PRACTICE A:

1. HABLAR

PRESENT	P. PERFECT	PRETERITE	IMPERFECT
hablo	he hablado	hablé	hablaba
hablas	has hablado	hablaste	hablabas
habla	ha hablado	habló	hablaba
hablamos	hemos hablado	hablamos	hablábamos
habláis	habéis hablado	hablasteis	hablabais
hablan	han hablado	hablaron	hablaban

2. PONER

PRESENT	P. PERFECT	PRETERITE	IMPERFECT
pongo	he puesto	puse	ponía
pones	has puesto	pusiste	ponías
pone	ha puesto	puso	ponía
ponemos	hemos puesto	pusimos	poníamos
ponéis	habéis puesto	pusisteis	poníais
ponen	han puesto	pusieron	ponían

3. ESTAR

PRESENT	P. PERFECT	PRETERITE	IMPERFECT
estoy	he estado	estuve	estaba
estás	has estado	estuviste	estabas
está	ha estado	estuvo	estaba
estamos	hemos estado	estuvimos	éstabamos
estáis	habéis estado	estuvisteis	estabais
están	han estado	estuvieron	estaban

4. SER

PRESENT	P. PERFECT	PRETERITE	IMPERFECT
soy	he sido	fui	era
eres	has sido	fuiste	eras
es	ha sido	fue	era
somos	hemos sido	fuimos	éramos
sois	habéis sido	fuisteis	erais
son	han sido	fueron	eran

5. LEER

PRESENT	P. PERFECT	PRETERITE	IMPERFECT
leo	he leido	leí	leía
lees	has leido	leiste	leías
lee	ha leido	leyó	leía
leemos	hemos leido	leimos	leíamos
leéis	habéis leido	leisteis	leíais
leen	han leido	leyeron	leían

6. SUBIR

PRESENT	P. PERFECT	PRETERITE	IMPERFECT
subo	he subido	subí	subía
subes	has subido	subiste	subías
sube	ha subido	subió	subía
subimos	hemos subido	subimos	subíamos
subís	habéis subido	subisteis	subíais
suben	han subido	subieron	subían

7. VOLVER

PRESENT	P. PERFECT	PRETERITE	IMPERFECT
vuelvo	he vuelto	volví	volvía
vuelves	has vuelto	volviste	volvías
vuelve	ha vuelto	volvió	volvía
volvemos	hemos vuelto	volvimos	volvíamos
volvéis	habéis vuelto	volisteis	volvíais
vuelven	han vuelto	volvieron	volvían

8. IR

PRESENT	P. PERFECT	PRETERITE	IMPERFECT
voy	he ido	fui	iba
vas	has ido	fuiste	ibas
va	ha ido	fue	iba
vamos	hemos ido	fuimos	íbamos
vais	habéis ido	fuisteis	ibais
van	han ido	fueron	iban

9. CANTAR

PRESENT	P. PERFECT	PRETERITE	IMPERFECT
canto	he cantado	canté	cantaba
cantas	has cantado	cantaste	cantabas
canta	ha cantado	cantó	cantaba
cantamos	hemos cantado	cantamos	cantábamos
cantáis	habéis cantado	cantasteis	cantabais
cantan	han cantado	cantaron	cantaban

10. QUERER

PRESENT	P. PERFECT	PRETERITE	IMPERFECT
quiero	he querido	quise	quería
quieres	has querido	quisiste	querías
quiere	ha querido	quiso	quería
queremos	hemos querido	quisimos	queríamos
queréis	habéis querido	quisisteis	queríais
quieren	han querido	quisieron	querían

11. PODER

PRESENT	P. PERFECT	PRETERITE	IMPERFECT
puedo	he podido	pude	podía
puedes	has podido	pudiste	podías
puede	ha podido	pudo	podía
podemos	hemos podido	pudimos	podíamos
podéis	habéis podido	pudisteis	podíais
pueden	han podido	pudieron	podían

12. TENER

PRESENT	P. PERFECT	PRETERITE	IMPERFECT
tengo	he tenido	tuve	tenía
tienes	has tenido	tuviste	tenías
tiene	ha tenido	tuvo	tenía
tenemos	hemos tenido	tuvimos	teníamos
tenéis	habéis tenido	tuvisteis	teníais
tienen	han tenido	tuvieron	tenían

Copyright© Vicki Marie Riley 1999-2023. All rights reserved.

13. MIRAR

PRESENT	P. PERFECT	PRETERITE	IMPERFECT
miro	he mirado	miré	miraba
miras	has mirado	miraste	mirabas
mira	ha mirado	miró	miraba
miramos	hemos mirado	miramos	mirábamos
miráis	habéis mirado	mirasteis	mirababais
miran	han mirado	miraron	mirababan

14. ABRIR

PRESENT	P. PERFECT	PRETERITE	IMPERFECT
abro	he abierto	abrí	abría
abres	has abierto	abriste	abrías
abre	ha abierto	abrió	abría
abrimos	hemos abierto	abrimos	abríamos
abrís	habéis abierto	abristeis	abríais
abren	han abierto	abrieron	abrían

15. LEVANTARSE

PRESENT	P. PERFECT	PRETERITE	IMPERFECT
me levanto	me he levantado	me levanté	me levantaba
te levantas	te has levantado	te levantaste	te levantabas
se levanta	se ha levantado	se levantó	se levantaba
nos levantamos	nos hemos levantado	nos levantamos	nos levantábamos
os levantáis	os habéis levantado	os levantáis	os levantabais
se levantan	se han levantado	se levantaron	se levantaban

16. ACOSTARSE

PRESENT	P. PERFECT	PRETERITE	IMPERFECT
me acuesto	me he acostado	me acosté	me acostaba
te acuestas	te has acostado	te acostaste	te acostabas
se acuesta	se ha acostado	se acostó	se acostaba
nos acostamos	nos hemos acostado	nos acostamos	nos acostábamos
os acostáis	os habéis acostado	os acostasteis	os acostabais
se acuestan	se han acostado	se acostaron	se acostaban

17. DECIR

PRESENT	P. PERFECT	PRETERITE	IMPERFECT
digo	he dicho	dije	decía
dices	has dicho	dijiste	decías
dice	ha dicho	dijo	decía
decimos	hemos dicho	dijimos	decíamos
decís	habéis dicho	dijisteis	decíais
dicen	han dicho	dijeron	decían

18. VENIR

PRESENT	P. PERFECT	PRETERITE	IMPERFECT
vengo	he venido	vine	venía
vienes	has venido	viniste	venías
viene	ha venido	vino	venía
venimos	hemos venido	vinimos	veníamos
venís	habéis venido	vinisteis	veníais
vienen	han venido	vinieron	venían

19. LLEVAR

PRESENT	P. PERFECT	PRETERITE	IMPERFECT
llevo	he llevado	llevé	llevaba
llevas	has llevado	llevaste	llevabas
lleva	ha llevado	llevó	llevaba
llevamos	hemos llevado	llevamos	llevábamos
lleváis	habéis llevado	llevasteis	llevabais
llevan	han llevado	llevaron	llevaban

20. PENSAR

PRESENT	P. PERFECT	PRETERITE	IMPERFECT
pienso	he pensado	pensé	pensaba
piensas	has pensado	pensaste	pensabas
piensa	ha pensado	pensó	pensaba
pensamos	hemos pensado	pensamos	pensábamos
pensáis	habéis pensado	pensasteis	pensabais
piensan	han pensado	pensaron	pensaban

26. COMPARISON OF TENSES.

PRACTICE A: (FREE ANSWERS)

1. HACER

¿Qué haces los sábados?
¿Qué has hecho hoy?
¿Qué hiciste el sábado?
¿Qué hacías el sábado por la mañana?

2. LEVANTARSE

¿A qué hora te levantas normalmente?
¿A qué hora te levantaste ayer?
¿A qué hora te levantabas?
¿A qué hora te has levantado esta mañana?

3. IR

¿Adónde vas de compras?
¿Adónde has ido hoy?
¿Adónde fuiste anteayer?
¿Adónde ibas los domingos?

4. HABLAR

¿Cuántos idiomas hablas?
¿Con quién has hablado hoy?
¿Hablaste con alguien por teléfono anoche?
¿Hablabas con alguien por teléfono el domingo?

5. PONER/COMPRAR

¿Dónde pones tus/las llaves?
¿Dónde has puesto tu diccionario?
¿Dónde pusiste la última cosa que compraste?
¿Dónde ponías la ropa?

6. ESCRIBIR

¿Escribes muchos emails?
¿Has escrito algo para una revista?
¿Escribiste a tu familia la semana pasada?
¿Escribías muchas cartas antes del internet?

7. ESTAR

¿Dónde estuviste el domingo?
¿Estabas a menudo en el cine en Gran Bretaña?
¿Has estado en Méjico alguna vez?
¿Dónde estás?

8. SER

¿Has sido estudiante alguna vez?
¿De dónde eres?
¿Cómo fue tu último cumpleaños?
¿De dónde era tu último profesor de español?

9. BEBER

¿Qué bebiste anoche antes de cenar/la cena?
¿Qué bebes por la mañana?
¿Qué bebías en un restaurante?
¿Has bebido café hoy?

10. ESTUDIAR

¿Qué estudias?
¿Has estudiado mucho este mes?
¿Qué estudiaste el año pasado?
¿Dónde estudiabas el año pasado?

27. IDIOMATIC EXPRESSIONS

PRACTICE A:

1: 6.
2: 1.
3: 2.
4: 7.
5: 16.
6: 3.
7: 10.
8: 15.
9: 5.
10: 12.

11: 13.
12: 4.
13: 14.
14: 8.
15: 11.
16: 9

PRACTICE B:

1. El hermano de Juan bebe como una esponja.
2. Llovía a cántaros mientras estábamos en Galicia.
3. Carmen era persona que siempre veía todo con malos ojos.
4. El hijo de María tiene 14 años. Está en la edad de pavo.
5. Siempre pago el pato para él.
6. Cuando eran niños siempre estaban de uñas.
7. Cuando Pedro se levantó el domingo pasado tuvo un humor de perros.
8. Pienso que ha perdido los papeles.
9. Tio Frank siempre era un viejo verde.
10. Se ha recuperado. Es de pasta dura.
11. Es bastante guapo, pero no es plato de mi gusto.
12. No tuvimos ganas de estudiar ayer entonces nos fumamos una clase.
13. No pudo comprender/entender que dije porque no tiene luces.
14. Ganaron la lotería la semana pasada. Siempre han tenido buena estrella.
15. Siempre andaba con cien ojos cuando estaba él, me daba mala espina.

28. LA ACTRÍZ ESTRELLA FUGAZ

PRACTICE A:

VERB	INFINITIVE	ENGLISH	TENSE	PERSON
1. era	ser	To be	imperfect	3rd p.sing.
2. vivía	vivir	To live	imperfect	3rd p.sing
3. llevó	llevar	To take	preterite	3rd p.sing
4. dar	dar	To give	infinitive	
5. cruzó	cruzar	To cross	preterite	3rd p.sing
6. Fue	ser	To be	preterite	3rd p.sing
7. impresionó	impresionar	To impress	preterite	3rd p.sing
8. empezó	empezar	To start	preterite	3rd p.sing
9. trabajar	trabajar	To work	infinitive	

10. decidió	decidir	To decide	preterite	3rd p.sing
11. llamarse	llamarse	To call (herself)	infinitive	
12. es	ser	To be	present	3rd p.sing
13. dice	decir	To say	present	3rd p.sing
14. es	ser	To be	present	3rd p.sing
15. son	ser	To be	present	3rd p.plural
16. es	ser	To be	present	3rd p.sing
17. sigue	seguir	To continue	present	3rd p.sing
18. ha sido	ser	To be	present perfect	3rd p.sing
19. es	ser	To be	present	3rd p.sing
20. se enamora	enamorarse	To fall in love	present	3rd p.sing
21. deja	dejar	To leave	present	3rd p.sing
22. amar	amar	To love	infinitive	
23. llevó	llevar	To take	preterite	3rd p.sing
24. empezó	empezar	To start	preterite	3rd p.sing
25. se durmió	dormirse	To fall asleep	preterite	3rd p.sing
26. se despertó	despertarse	To wake up	preterite	3rd p.sing
27. preguntó	preguntar	To ask	preterite	3rd p.sing
28. gusta	gustar	To like	present	3rd p.sing
29. sonrió	sonreir	To smile	preterite	3rd p.sing
30. dijo	decir	To say	preterite	3rd p.sing
31. ver	ver	To see	infinitive	
32. hacer	hacer	To do	infinitive	
33. necesito	necesitar	To need	present	1st p.sing
34. venir	venir	To come	infinitive	
35. dice	decir	To say	present	3rd p.sing
36. es	ser	To be	present	3rd p.sing
37. ha conocido	conocer	To know	present perfect	3rd p.sing
38. era	ser	To be	imperfect	3rd p.sing
39. se parecía	parecerse	To be like	imperfect	3rd p.sing

PRACTICE B:

When she was small she lived in the countryside. One summer night her father took her for a walk. Suddenly, a star crossed the sky from one side to the other. It was a shooting star. That impressed her a lot, and because of that, when she started to work in films, she decided to call herself Shooting Star.

Currently Star is one of the richest andmost famous women in the world, but she says that for her money isn´t important. More important are her career, he little dog Light and love.

Although she is rich and beautiful, she is still single. She has always been lucky but she is very fickle in love. She falls in love easily and falls out of love just as easily.

She took her sixty-year old grandmother to the premiere of her latest film. As soon as the film started her grandmother fell asleep and didn´t wake up until the end.

Star asked her- Grandmother, don´t you like my film?

Her grandmother smiled and said- I don´t have to come to the cinema to watch you act silly!!-

Star says that her grandmother is one of the most intelligent women she has met, and that when she was young she looked/ was/ seemed a lot like her.

PRACTICE C:

1. ¿Dónde vivía Estrella cuando era pequeña? Vivía en el campo.
2. ¿Adónde la llevó su padre una noche? La llevó a dar un paseo.
3. ¿Qué pasó de repente? Una estrella cruzó el cielo de un lado a otro.
4. ¿Cómo se llamó cuando empezó a trabajar en el cine? Decidió llamarse "Estrella Fugaz".
5. ¿Cómo es ella? Es una de las mujeres más ricas y famosas del mundo,
6. ¿Es importante el dinero? Dice que no.
7. ¿Está casada? No, sigue soltera.
8. ¿A quién llevó al estreno de su última película? Llevó a su abuela de sesenta años
9. ¿Qué hizo en cuanto empezó la película? La abuela se durmió.
10. ¿Cuándo se despertó? No se despertó hasta el final.
11. ¿Qué dijo la abuela cuando le preguntó se le gusto la película? Dijo- Para verte hacer tonterías, no necesito venir al cine.
12. ¿Qué dice Estrella sobre su abuela? Estrella dice que su abuela es una de las mujeres más inteligentes que ha conocido, y que cuando su abuela era joven se parecía mucho a ella.

29. THE PAST PERFECT (PLUPERFECT OR "PLUSCAMPERFECTO")

PRACTICE A:

1. Escribir - to write   - escrito - written.
2. Hacer –   to do/ make   - hecho – done/ made
3. Romper – to break   - roto - broken
4. Ver -   to see   - visto – seen
5. Volver - to return   - vuelto – returned
6. Decir – to say/ tell   - dicho – said/ told
7. Abrir -   to open   - abierto - opened
8. Morir - to die   - muerto – died
9. Poner – to put   - puesto - put
10. Cubrir - to cover   - cubierto - covered
11. Freir – to fry   - frito - frito

PRACTICE B:

1. Ya habia limpiado el coche cuando empezó a llover.
2. Cuando llegamos a casa no había hecho nada.
3. Cuando volvieron a casa todas las flores habían muerto.
4. Yo había puesto el dinero en el cajón y después alguien llamó a la puerta.
5. Él la había llamado por lo menos diez veces antes de salir.
6. No pude instalar el programa porque la tienda no me había dado bastante información.
7. Los ladrones habían roto todas las puertas y ventanas.
8. Cuando fui a trabajar a las siete todavía no habían encontrado las llaves para entrar.
9. Habíamos abierto todas las ventanas porque hizo calor.
10. No quise ir al cine porque ya había visto la película.
11. Cuando le ví no había dicho nada a Carmen.
12. Habían escrito veinte correos electrónicos antes de recibir una respuesta.
13. Yo había pagado el florero, entonces lo tire y lo rompí.
14. Habíamos vivido en muchos otros paises antes de venir a España.
15. Incluso el día antes todavía no habían recibido la invitación.
16. Ella no le había vistoSanteds del día de su boda.
17. No estaba/ estuve nervioso porque había practicado el discurso por/

durante dos horas la noche antes.
18. ¿Habías limpiado la casa antes de la fiesta?
19. No habíais apagado las luces antes de salir de la oficina anoche
20. No habían hecho nada toda la semana.

PRACTICE C:

Nunca habíamos estado en Francia antes aunque habíamos viajado mucho en el resto de Europa. Mi marido siempre había querido ir a París y había Ganado bastante dinero en la lotería, entonces decidimos ir y quedarnos en un hotel en el centro de la ciudad. Antes de salir, habíamos comprador nuevas maletas, mucha ropa, y dos pares de gafas de sol caras. También habíamos comprador un Ipad para que podíamos/ pudimos sacar/tomar muchas photos, y habíamos pedido a nuestros vecinos cuidar a nuestros dos gatos. El día que salimos para el aeropuerto el col brillaba/ brilló y estuvimos/ estabamos felices/ contentos que habíamos preparado todo y pudimos descansar y disfrutar de nuestras vacaciones.

31. COMPARISON OF TENSES/ ENGLISH TO SPANISH 1.

PRACTICE A:

VERB	INFINITIVE	SPANISH	TENSE	PERSON
1. we left	To leave	salir	preterite	1st p.plural
2. returned	To return	volver	preterite	1st p.plural
3. was	To be	estar	imperfect	3rd p. sing
4. was	To be	estar	imperfect	3rd p. sing
5. we saw	To see	ver	preterite	1st p.plural
6. he was walking	To walk	andar	imperfect	3rd p. sing
7. was	To be	Tener (age)	imperfect	3rd p. sing
8. was carrying	To carry	llevar	imperfect	3rd p. sing
9. we stopped	To stop	parar	preterite	1st p.plural
10. asked	To ask	preguntar	preterite	1st p.plural
11. was going	To go	ir	imperfect	3rd p. sing
12. explained	To explain	explicar	preterite	3rd p. sing
13. he had found	To find	encontrar	past perfect	3rd p. sing
14. opened	To open	abrir	preterite	3rd p. sing
15. found	To find	encontrar	preterite	3rd p. sing
16. was going	To go	ir	imperfect	3rd p. sing

17. he got into	To get into	subir	preterite	3rd p. sing
18. we took	To take	llevar	preterite	1st p.plural
19. he gave	To give	dar	preterite	3rd p. sing

PRACTICE B:

Ayer por la tarde salimos del hotel acerca de/ sobre las seis y media y volvimos/ regresamos al hotel en nuestro coche. Nuestro hotel estaba en el pueblo sobre cinco kilómetros de la playa y el hotel de nuestro amigo estaba dos kilómetros más lejos. En nuestro camino al pueblo vimos un pescador mayor/ viejo, andaba lentamente por la carretera. Tenía más o menos setenta años y llevaba una caja grande en (su/ la) mano. Paramos el coche y le preguntamos a donde iba. Nos explicó que había encontrado la caja en la arena cerca de su barca de pescar.
Cuando la abrió encontró algunos papeles y también un sobre con miles de euros. Ahora iba a la estación de policía/ Comisaria en el pueblo. Subió en el coche y lo llevamos a la estación de policía/ Comisaria donde dio todo al policía.

PRACTICE C:

1. ¿Cuádo salieron de la playa? Sobre las seis y media.
2. ¿Cómo volvieron/ regresaron al hotel? Volvieron/ salieron en coche.
3. ¿ ¿Dónde estaba el hotel? Estaba en el pueblo sobre cinco kilómetros de la playa
4. ¿Dónde estaba el hotel de su amigo? Estaba dos kilómetros más lejos.
5. ¿Qué vieron en su camino al pueblo? Un pescador mayor/ viejo que andaba lentamente por la carretera.
6. ¿Cuántos años tenía? Tenía más o menos setenta años.
7. ¿Qué llevaba en su/ la mano? Llevaba una caja grande en (su/ la) mano.
8. ¿Qué hicieron entonces? Pararon el coche y le preguntaron a donde iba.
9. ¿Dónde había encontrado la caja? Había encontrado la caja en la arena cerca de su barca de pescar.
10. ¿Qué encontró cuando la abrió? Encontró algunos papeles y también un sobres con miles de euros.
11. ¿Qué hacía ahora? Ahora iba a la estación de policía/ Comisaria en el pueblo
12. ¿Dónde lo llevaron? Lo llevaron a la estación de policía/ Comisaria.

13. ¿Qué hizo allí? Dio todo al policía.
14. ¿Alguna vez has encontrado algo raro? *FREE ANSWER*
15. ¿Qué hiciste? *FREE ANSWER*

32. COMPARISON OF TENSES/ ENGLISH TO SPANISH 2.

PRACTICE A:

Verb in context	Infinitive	Spanish	Tense	Person
1. we were	To be	estar	preterite	1st p.plural
2. we spent	To spend	pasar	preterite	1st p.plural
3. had we arrived	To arrive	llegar	past perfect	1st p.plural
4. we were going to	To go	ir	imperfect	1st p.plural
5. stay	To stay	quedarse	infinitive	
6. told	To tell	decir	preterite	3rd p. sing
7. were going to	To go	ir	imperfect	3rd p.plural
8. pass	To pass	pasar	infinitive	
9. I had seen	To see	ver	past perfect	1st p. sing
10. were	To be	estar	Pret or imp	3rd p.plural
11. we all got up	To get up	levantarse	preterite	1st p.plural
12. to see	To see	ver	infinitive	
13. we arrived	To arrive	llegar	preterite	1st p.plural
14. we found	To find	encontrar	preterite	1st p.plural
15. waiting	To wait	esperar	gerund	
16. we waited	To wait	esperar	preterite	1st p.plural
17. there was	There is	haber	imperfect	3rd p. sing
18. appeared	To appear	aparecer	preterite	3rd p.plural
19. they had all gone	To go	ir	past perfect	3rd p.plural
20. went	To go	ir	preterite	3rd p. sing
21. to talk	To talk	hablar	infinitive	
22. they had seen	To see	ver	past perfect	3rd p.plural
23. had happened	To happen	pasar	past perfect	3rd p. sing
24. seemed	To seem	parecer	preterite	3rd p. sing
25. to be	To be	estar	infinitive	
26. we watched	To watch	mirar/ver	preterite	1st p.plural
27. we saw	To see	ver	preterite	1st p.plural
28. pass	To pass	pasar	infinitive	
29. we saw	To see	ver	preterite	1st p.plural

PRACTICE B:

Cuando estuvimos en España el año pasado pasamos una noche en un pueblo pequeño en las montañas cerca de Madrid. Apenas habíamos llegado cuando el dueño del hotel donde íbamos a quedarnos nos dijo que el día siguiente los ciclistas en la Vuelta de España iban a pasar por el pueblo.

Yo había visto la carrera antes, pero mis amigos estaban muy interesados entonces todos nos levantamos muy tempranos para verla. Sin embargo, cuando llegamos a la Plaza Principal encontramos una multitud enorme ya esperando la llegada de los ciclistas. Esperamos mucho tiempo pero hubo mucha emoción cuando al final aparecieron los líderes.

Pronto todos habían ido y todo el mundo fue a los bares para hablar de lo que habían visto. Nada sensacional había pasado pero todo el mundo pareció muy animado. Por la tarde, vimos/ miramos un programa especial en la tele y vimos a los ciclistas pasar por la Plaza Principal de camino a Madrid. i!Nos vimos también!!

PRACTICE C:

1. ¿Cuándo estuvieron en España? El año pasado.
2. ¿Dónde pasaron una noche? Pasaron una noche en un pueblo pequeño en las montañas cerca de Madrid.
3. ¿Qué les dijo el dueño del hotel donde iban a quedarse? Les dijo que el día siguiente los ciclistas en la Vuelta de España iban a pasar por el pueblo
4. ¿Quién había visto la carrera antes? El narrador había visto la carrera antes
5. ¿Qué hicieron para verla? Se levantaron muy tempranos para verla.
6. ¿Qué encontraron cuando llegaron a la Plaza Principal? Encontraron una multitud enorme ya esperando la llegada de los ciclistas
7. ¿Tuvieron que esperar mucho tiempo? Sí. tuvieron que esperar mucho tiempo.
8. ¿Qué hizo todo el mundo después de todos habían ido? Todo el mundo fue a los bares para hablar de lo que habían visto
9. ¿Cómo estuvo todo el mundo? Todo el mundo pareció muy animado.
10. ¿ Qué miraron/ vieron aquella/ esa tarde? Vieron/ miraron un programa especial en la tele.
11. ¿A quiénes vieron/ miraron también? Se vieron/ miraron también.
12. ¿Alguna vez has visto un evento Famoso? Escribe sobre ello.

33. PRACTICE OF PAST TENSES, "ADIÓS MARÍA".

PRACTICE A:

VERB	INFINITIVE	ENGLISH	TENSE	PERSON
1. estudiaba	estudiar	To study	imperfect	3rd p. sing
2. asistía	asistir	To attend	imperfect	3rd p. sing
3. cenar	cenar	To dine	infinitive	
4. practicaba	practicar	To practice	imperfect	3rd p. sing
5. practicaba	practicar	To practice	imperfect	3rd p. sing
6. molestaba	molestar	To annoy	imperfect	3rd p. sing
7. podían	poder	To be able	imperfect	3rd p. plural
8. dormir	dormir	To sleep	infinitive	
9. se indignaban	indignarse	To get angry	imperfect	3rd p. plural
10. tenían	tener	To have	imperfect	3rd p. plural
11. era	ser	To be	imperfect	3rd p. sing
12. se consideraba	considerarse	To consider	imperfect	3rd p. sing
13. era	ser	To be	imperfect	3rd p. sing
14. Llegó	llegar	To arrive	preterite	3rd p. sing
15. abrían	abrir	To open	imperfect	3rd p. plural
16. combatir	combatir	To combat	infinitive	
17. oían	oir	To hear	imperfect	3rd p. plural
18. gritaban	gritar	To shout	imperfect	3rd p. plural
19. Queremos	querer	To want	present	1st p. plural
20. dormir	dormir	To sleep	infinitive	
21. es	ser	To be	present	3rd p. sing
22. aprobó	aprobar	To pass	preterite	3rd p. sing
23. concedieron	conceder	To award	preterite	3rd p. plural
24. ampliar	ampliar	To extend	infinitive	
25. partir	partir	To leave	infinitive	
26. dieron	dar	To give	preterite	3rd p. plural
27. celebraron	celebrar	To celebrate	preterite	3rd p. plural
28. Bebieron	beber	To drink	preterite	3rd p. plural
29. bailaron	bailar	To dance	preterite	3rd p. plural
30. duró	durar	To last	preterite	3rd p. sing
31. bailaban	bailar	To dance	imperfect	3rd p. plural
32. cantaban	cantar	To sing	imperfect	3rd p. plural
33. aplaudían	aplaudir	To applaud	imperfect	3rd p. plural

PRACTICE B.

María Garcia was studying intensively to be a piano player. During the day she attended Music School and at night, after dinner, she practised/ used to practice at home on her own piano. Often Marlia practised until one or two in the morning. This annoyed the neighbours. Some couldn´t sleep and got angry/indignant. Besides, the neighbours did not like her mother Carmen. Carmen Garcia was from a noble family and considered herself superior the the rest/ other of the inhabitants in the street. She was a very proud woman.

Summer arrived and at night the neighbours would open their windows to combat the heat. But then they could hear María´s piano more loudly. The neighbour would shout/ used to shout-
We want to sleep! You have no right! This is abuse!
María passed her exams with the maximum grades and was awarded a grant to extend her studies in Vienna. The night before leaving for that City, the mother and her daughter gave a farewell party for their family and friends.
At the same time, all the neighbours of the street celebrated with a big dinner. They drank a lot of champagne and danced. The fun lasted until daybreak/ dawn and the neighbours were dancing, singing and applauding. At the end, they were all shouting-
Goodbye Maria, goodbye!!

PRACTICE C.

1. ¿Qué estudiaba María? María García estudiaba intensamente la carrera de piano.
2. ¿Qué hacía durante el día? Durante el día asistía el Conservatorio.
3. ¿Qué hacía después de cenar? Practicaba en casa en su piano particular.
4. ¿Hasta qué hora practicaba a menudo? Hasta la una o las dos de la madrugada.
5. ¿Por qué molestaba esto a los vecinos? Porque algunos no podían dormir y se indignaban.
6. ¿Por qué tenían los vecinos mucha antipatía a la madre de María, Carmen?
   Porque Carmen García era de familia noble y se consideraba superior a todos los demás habitantes de la calle.
7. ¿Cómo era? Era una señora muy orgullosa.
8. ¿Qué pasó cuando llegó el verano? Por la noche todos los vecinos abrían las ventanas para combatir el calor.

9. ¿Por qué gritaban los vecinos? Porque oían el piano de María con más fuerza.
10. ¿Aprobó María los exámenes? Si, los aprobó con la máxima nota.
11. ¿Dónde iba a estudiar? Iba a estudiar en Viena.
12. ¿Qué hicieron María y su madre la noche antes de partir? Dieron una fiesta de despedida a sus familiares y amigos.
13. ¿Qué hicieron los vecinos a la vez? Celebraron con una cena grande.
14. ¿Hasta qué hora duró la diversión? La diversión duró hasta el amanecer.
15. ¿Qué hacían los vecinos? Bailaban, cantaban y aplaudían.
16. ¿Qué gritaban al final? -Adiós María, adiós!!!

34. TRANSLATION FROM ENGLISH TO SPANISH- MIXED TENSES.

PRACTICE A:

VERB	INFINITIVE	SPANISH	TENSE	PERSON
1. I went	to go	ir	preterite	1st p.singular
2. I went	to go	ir	preterite	1st p.singular
3. I was	to be	estar	preterite	1st p.singular
4. I visited	to visit	visitar	preterite	1st p.singular
5. was	to be	estar	imperfect	3rd person singular.
6. was	to be	ser	imperfect	3rd person singular.
7. was	to be	estar	preterite	3rd person singular.
8. it did not rain	to rain	llover	preterite	3rd person singular.
9. I met	to meet	conocer	preterite	1st p.singular
10. I have never seen	to see	ver	present perfect	1st p.singular
11. I visited	to visit	visitar	preterite	1st p.singular
12. I went	to go	ir	preterite	1st p.singular
13. I stayed	to stay	quedarse	preterite	1st p.singular
14. I did not like	to like	gustar (to please)	preterite	1st p.singular
15. there were	============	haber	preterite	3rd person plural.
16. was	to be	ser	imperfect	3rd person singular.
17. was	to be	hacer	preterite	3rd person singular.

BREAK THE LANGUAGE BARRIER LEVEL 2
WWW.ELPRINCIPECENTRE.ORG
info@elprincipecentre.org

		(weather)		
18. I have seen	to see	ver	present perfect	1st p.singular
19. I do not want	to want	querer	present	1st p.singular
20. to return	to return	volver	infinitive	
21. I travelled	to travel	viajar	preterite	1st p.singular
22. I was	to be	estar	preterite	1st p.singular
23. was	to be	ser	imperfect	3rd person singular.
24. I had	to have	tener	preterite	1st p.singular
25. to see	to see	ver	infinitive	
26. I have always wanted	to want	querer	p.perfect	1st p.singular
27. to visit	to visit	visitar	infinitive	
28. I did not have	to have	tener	preterite	1st p.singular
29. I caught	to catch	coger	preterite	1st p.singular
30. was	to be	estar	preterite	1st person singular.
31. it rained	to rain	llover	preterite	3rd person singular.
32. I had	to have	pasar (to have a good time)	preterite	1st p.singular
33. I went	to go	ir	preterite	1st p.singular
34. it was	to be	ser	preterite	3rd person singular.
35. I have never paid	to pay	pagar	present perfect	1st p.singular
36. I went	to go	ir	preterite	1st p.singular
37. it was	to be	ser	imperfect	3rd person singular.
38. I have ever visited	to visit	visitar	present perfect	1st p.singular
39. I was	to be	estar	preterite	1st p.singular
40. was	to be	hacer (weather)	imperfect	3rd person singular.
41. I met up	to meet up	reunir	preterite	1st p.singular
42. live	to live	vivir	present	3rd person plural
43. we went	to go	ir	preterite	1st person plural
44. it was	to be	ser	imperfect	3rd person singular.
45. was	to be	ser	imperfect	3rd person singular.
46. were	to be	ser	imperfect	3rd person plural
47. we went	to go	ir	preterite	1st person plural
48. to see	to see	ver	infinitive	
49. we skied	to ski	esquiar	preterite	1st person plural

Copyright© Vicki Marie Riley 1999-2023. All rights reserved.

50. was	to be	ser	preterite	3rd person singular.
51. I went	to go	ir	preterite	1st p.singular
52. I did	to do	hacer	preterite	1st p.singular
53. I have never studied	to study	estudiar	p. perfect	1st p.singular
54. I found	to find	encontrar	preterite	1st p.singular
55. were	to be	ser	imperfect	3rd person plural
56. I made	to make	hacer	preterite	1st p.singular
57. I returned	to return	volver	preterite	1st p.singular
58. I have had	to have	tener	p. perfect	1st p.singular

PRACTICE B:

Hace unas semanas fui de vacaciones a España. Primero fui a Barcelona donde estuve durante tres días.

Visité todos los sitios/lugares interesantes. El hotel estaba cerca de "Las Ramblas" y era muy cómodo. Estuvo un poco nublado, pero no llovió. Conocí a mucha gente simpática/muchas personas simpáticas allí y nunca he visto edificios tan bonitos.

Después de Barcelona, visité Palma de Mallorca. Fui en barco y me quedé allí durante diez días. No me gustó mucho porque habían muchos turistas y el apartamento era muy ruidoso. Hizo muy mal tiempo también. Sin embargo, ya lo he visto pero no quiero volver.

Desde Palma, viajé por avión a Valencia. Estuve allí solo dos días. El hotel era muy incómodo y tuve muy poco tiempo para ver la ciudad. Siempre he querido visitar el Museo de Ciencias, pero no tuve tiempo.

Cogí el tren a Madrid y estuve allí durante siete días. Aunque llovió durante cuatro días lo pasé muy bien. Fui al Museo del Prado, el estadio de fútbol Bernabeu, el Parque del Retiro y muchos otros sitios/lugares, pero fue muy caro. Nunca he pagado tanto dinero por una taza de café.

Después fui a Granada en autobús. Era el sitio más bonito que nunca he visitado. Estuve allí seis días, hizo muy buen tiempo, y me reuní con algunos amigos que viven allí. Fuimos al Palacio de Alhambra, era impresionante. La ciudad era muy bonita y la gente amable. Fuimos a ver un tablao flamenco y esquiamos en la Sierra Nevada. La nieve era muy bonita.

Finalmente, fui a Salamanca en coche donde hice un curso intensivo de español. Nunca he estudiado un idioma antes y lo encontré difícil pero interesante. Los profesores eran muy simpáticos, también los otros estudiantes. Hice muchos amigos y después de quince días volví a casa. He tenido una experiencia estupenda.

PRACTICE C:

1. ¿Cuándo fue de vacaciones? Fue de vacaciones hace unas semanas.
2. ¿Adónde fue primero? Primero fue a Barcelona.
3. ¿Cuánto tiempo estuvo allí? Estuvo allí durante tres días.
4. ¿Cómo era el hotel? El hotel era muy cómodo.
5. ¿Qué tiempo hizo? Estuvo un poco nublado, pero no llovió.
6. ¿A quién conoció? Conoció a mucha gente/muchas personas.
7. ¿Qué nunca ha visto? Nunca ha visto edificios tan bonitos.
8. ¿Adónde fue después? Después de Barcelona, visitó /fue a Palma de Mallorca.
9. ¿Cómo fue/llegó? Fue en barco.
10. ¿Cuánto tiempo estuvo allí? Se quedó/estuvo allí durante diez días.
11. ¿Le gustó? No le gustó mucho.
12. ¿Por qué? Porque habían muchos turistas y el apartamento era muy ruidoso.
13. ¿Adónde fue después y cómo? Después viajó por avión a Valencia/ fue a Valencia por avión.
14. ¿Qué siempre ha querido visitar? Siempre ha querido visitar el Museo de Ciencias.
15. ¿Cómo fue/llegó a Madrid? Cogió el tren a Madrid
16. ¿Lo pasó bien? Si, lo pasó muy bien.
17. ¿Cuánto tiempo estuvo en Granada? Estuvo en Granada seis días.
18. ¿Cómo era el Palacio del Alhambra? Era impresionante.
19. ¿Qué hicieron en la Sierra Nevada? Esquiaron.
20. ¿Cómo fue/llegó a Salamanca? Fue a Salamanca en coche.
21. ¿Qué hizo allí? Hizo un curso intensivo de español.
22. ¿Ha tenido una experiencia buena? Sí, ha tenido una experiencia estupenda.

www.ingramcontent.com/pod-product-compliance
Lightning Source LLC
Chambersburg PA
CBHW081346040426
42450CB00015B/3326